GOVERNMENT COLLISION

By

MARIOS ELLINAS

For Worldwide Distribution, Printed in the U.S.A.

ISBN: 978-0-615-63020-5

Government Collision

By Marios Ellinas

Printed by Createspace

Copyright 2012 — Marios A. Ellinas

www.mariosellinas.com

maellinas@yahoo.com

Cover Design by **Tulip Graphics**
tulipgr@mweb.co.za

FOREWORD

Government Collision, written by my dear friend, Marios Ellinas, is a book that brings timeless truth and revelation of God's Kingdom to life.

When God placed Marios and his wife, Danielle, in my life, it was one of those "Kingdom" moments that changed my life and ministry forever. Since that divine appointment in October, 2006, we have not only been friends but we have become family. Marios is one of the most humble, anointed, generous, loyal, men of God that I have ever met. He is a man led by the Holy Spirit who understands and operates in a governmental authority in the Kingdom of God. I have watched his life, been a guest in his home, and witnessed the love and passion for Christ that he and Danielle have imparted to their children. I have watched Marios navigate through transition, change, and the storms of life and ministry. He has operated in integrity through it all.

Marios has a keen understanding and insight into the things and ways of God, and has a unique ability to communicate the hidden truths and secrets of God in a very relevant and applicable way. Plainly put, Marios not only teaches about the Kingdom of God, he lives it out for the world to see.

The truth is that we are living in an unprecedented time in history where there seems to be a lack of absolute truth in the world and in the church. People seem to be living in a "grey" area that lacks conviction. It is more evident today than ever that there is a conflict of kingdoms between the Kingdom of God and the kingdom of darkness. It is in times like these we need a voice of truth, a beacon of light to expose the darkness and release the glory of Christ. God has raised up Marios Ellinas as one of those voices of truth and light.

Prepare to be challenged and changed as you experience the truths and revelation written on the pages of Government Collision. Marios ministers and writes out of a realm of rich revelation and spiritual truth. Over the past six years, I have had the honor of watching my friend, Marios, live out the things that he writes from his encounters with God. He has an amazing understanding and authority of the Kingdom and Government of God and presents it in a clear and real way in this book. This is one of the most timely and effective books for the hour in which we live!

David Wagner
Father's Heart Ministries
Pensacola, Florida

DEDICATION

To Jesus, the Author and Finisher

THANKS

Danielle, Christos, Caleb and Chloe for everything you are and mean to me—it would take volumes to express it, and I would be falling short, still.

To Mom and Dad, my brothers and Danielle's family for your continued encouragement and support. Thanks for buying my books and speaking encouragement.

To Valley Shore's amazing staff and congregation for passionately pursuing God's presence and His ways, without ever turning back.

To my mentors and close confidants, with whom I share life. You know who you are and how much you mean to me.

For the outstanding team of transcribers who served this project selflessly and sacrificially. Lori Cote, Denise Cote, Jillian Holmes, Michelle Kinrade, Alexandra Lefebvre, and Sinco Steendam—I am eternally grateful!

Peter Sylvester, for the servant's heart and high level of excellence, by which he formats all my manuscripts.

Jason Hackley and Danielle Ellinas for the painstaking work of editing the text.

David Wagner, for the *Foreword*, and many years of deep, genuine Kingdom friendship.

Tulip Graphics for always capturing the themes of my books in the cover design. Ronelle, you are amazing!

Contents

INTRODUCTION 13

Chapter 1: All About Jesus.................................25

Chapter 2: More Than a Prodigy 39

Chapter 3: Instant Credibility..............................53

Chapter 4: Shake-ups and Confrontations..............69

Chapter 5: Fearlessness Feared 83

Chapter 6: Increase and Relevance..........................99

Chapter 7: Crowd Control...................................115

Chapter 8: The Plot Unfolds 127

Chapter 9: Starting at the End..............................139

Epilogue Father, Holy Spirit… and Son! 151

INTRODUCTION

"He is blaspheming, claiming He is Christ, a king!"
"He is perverting the nation!"
"He has been misleading the people!"
"He is forbidding the Jews to pay the tribute tax to Caesar!"
"He made Himself the Son of God!"

Pontius Pilate was in a huge dilemma.

Before him was Jesus of Nazareth, accused by the Pharisees, scribes, chief priests and elders of the people. Voices raised, fingers pointing, faces frowned, and with great ferocity, Israel's ruling elite made their case.

Pilate's own judgment told him otherwise. The charges were weak, and he knew the priests' and elders' tactics all too well--much talk; no substance.

Moreover, unlike any criminal Pilate had faced before, Jesus was silent. Even when Pilate pressed for an answer whether He was King of the Jews, the accused answered simply and peacefully:

It is as you say.

His calm demeanor evoked wonder. Even His one response revealed a depth of character and internal spiritual strength.

Everything about Him silently, yet firmly, affirmed His innocence. Pilate announced a preliminary decision:

I find no fault in this Man.

That only made things worse. The prosecution turned up the heat:

He stirs up the people, teaching throughout all Judea, beginning from Galilee to this place! Luke 23:3-5.

Did someone say, *Galilee*?

Suddenly, through all the commotion and shouting, Pilate found an out. Jesus came from Nazareth of Galilee, a region beyond Pilate's jurisdiction. It was great news. Pilate promptly sent Jesus to Herod. The dilemma seemed to be over.

It wasn't!

Herod didn't want the case either. Perhaps it was due to the great commotion by the chief priests and scribes, who "stood and vehemently accused Him." Maybe it was Herod's disappointment when Jesus wouldn't perform a miracle for him to witness. It could be that the defendant's complete silence throughout all the proceedings infuriated the governor of Galilee. Whatever the cause, Herod was out. He and his soldiers had a last go at lambasting Jesus, and then Herod "sent Him back to Pilate." (Luke 23:10-11)

Pilate's dilemma returned, and things were rapidly getting worse. A crowd had gathered outside. Israel's statesmen were pushing for a verdict. Yet, nothing had happened to change Pilate's perception of Jesus—He was still innocent. The governor's own wife had even come to him, speaking of her troubling dream and warning him to "have nothing to do with that just Man." (Matthew 27:19)

Pilate sat on his judgment seat looking for another solution. It was the custom to release one prisoner to the Jews during the time of their feast. Pilate offered to release Jesus. He got nowhere, fast!

> *They all cried out at once, saying, "Away with this Man, and release to us Barabbas"* Luke 23:18

The issue was getting the best of the governor. The incited crowd was quickly turning into a mob, roaring against him. The chief priests intensified their intimidation:

> *If you let this Man go, you are not Caesar's friend. Whoever makes himself king speaks against Caesar!* John 19:12

Pilate had heard enough. He walked over to a basin, washed his hands, and self-proclaimed his innocence in the matter. Then, facing the crowd, he exclaimed:

> *Behold your King!*

The mob roared back:

> *Away with Him, away with Him! Crucify Him!*

Pilate made one last-ditched effort:

> *Shall I crucify your King?*

The answer did not come from the people this time, but from the crowd's key instigators:

The chief priests answered, "We have no king but Caesar!" John 19:14-16

Pilate found no more words. The vice had closed in on him.

[He] gave sentence that it should be as they requested... He released Barabbas to them; and when he had scourged Jesus, he delivered Him to be crucified. Matthew 27:26

Thus, Pontius Pilate, Roman governor of Judea, representing the most prominent and powerful government of the day, ordered the execution of Jesus Christ, God's only Son.

~~~

Everyone born in this world will eventually die; it is a fact of life. We enter the realm of this earth through the womb; we journey through various stages of development and accomplishment; then at some point, death terminates our time here, and we are ushered into eternity.

Jesus was the only human who arrived in the world with the assignment to die *for* the world. Long before Mary wrapped her baby in "swaddling cloths and laid Him in a manger," Jesus had been marked for death. When the Apostle John was taken up into heaven to witness "the things which are, and the things which will take place," he saw an image of Jesus as "The Lamb, slain from the foundation of the world." (Revelation 13:8)

Jesus' mission from the Father was to become the necessary ransom for the sins of humanity; He was marked for death in heaven from the beginning of time; however, to die in disgrace and dishonor as a common thief would not be God's doing, but men's.

Everything about Jesus' arrest, conviction, sentencing and execution was wrong, when He had only done right, every moment of every day throughout His life. For three years, Jesus walked the dusty roads of Galilee, Judea and Samaria, releasing life and restoring hope.

> *He went through every city and village, preaching and bringing the glad tidings of the kingdom of God.*
> Luke 8:1

Jesus healed every sick person brought to Him. He approached and brought freedom to society's outcasts, such as those who were demon-possessed and the "untouchable" lepers. He fed the hungry, gave to the poor, taught and modeled life-transforming principles. He personified integrity and sound leadership.

How could someone as benevolent and wholesome as Jesus end up standing before Pilate to be judged? How could He be nailed to a cross at Golgotha, next to thieves? The truth had to be twisted, lies had to be planted, bribes had to be granted—all part of a devious, multi-faceted conspiracy which began almost immediately after Jesus started His public ministry.

A partnership formed between Israel's spiritual and political powerbrokers, members of the Roman government, and a spirit from the realm of darkness, "the spirit of the Antichrist, which you have heard was coming, and is now already in the world." (1 John 4:3)

~~~

More than seven hundred years before Jesus was born, the prophet Isaiah foretold His coming:

For unto us a Child is born, Unto us a Son is given and the government shall be upon His shoulder.
Isaiah 9:6

Interestingly, Isaiah's prophecy made no reference to Jesus' ministry or way of life. Nothing about His masterful teaching, His miraculous works, His power over creation, the signs and wonders He would perform, or His flawless character. Isaiah simply said, a Child would be coming and He would be carrying "the government."

Earthly governments, as peculiar as they may have been throughout various times and places, have generally functioned as systems of law and administration, by which political areas are ruled. The government on Jesus' shoulder was not devised on earth, but in heaven. It was God's government – the form or system of rule, by which God rules. Everything Jesus was and did on the earth was in alignment and accordance with that government.

When God created Adam and Eve, He gave them and mankind the assignment to "fill the earth and subdue it." God told Adam and Eve to "have dominion" over everything else He created (Genesis 1:28). The couple was able to fulfill their responsibility of exercising dominion, because God delegated to them the necessary power and authority for the task. They were carriers of His government.

As long as Adam, Eve and their descendants obeyed God and operated within the confines of His authority systems, they would have dominion.

When Adam and Eve were seduced by satan (I remind the reader that the enemy's name is deliberately not capitalized throughout this work), and fell into sin, they forfeited their authority and lost their inheritance. Upon confronting their disobedience, and pronouncing judgment, God also announced the plan by which He would save man from sin, and restore him as carrier of His government and executor of dominion.

The plan required Jesus, the beloved Son of God, to leave the glorious realms of heaven and come to the earth as a man. He would live like us. He would go through the various stages of human development and face the same challenges, trials and temptations. Jesus would humble Himself, wholeheartedly serving all people. He would demonstrate the Kingdom of God, always operating from and releasing the most integral force in God's government, unconditional love.

Remaining obedient to His Father's will, Jesus would then endure betrayal, abandonment, rejection and false accusation. He would suffer in the hands of vicious persecutors, such as the Jewish rulers, and self-preserving politicians, such as Pilate. He would yield to a verdict from the most corrupt and ungodly government of His day, Rome, and would carry a cross on His back to the place of His execution.

The plan would culminate with Jesus' death on the cross. The Messiah would take upon Himself the weight of mankind's sins. Three days later, God would raise Jesus from the dead. He would obtain victory over satan, once and for all. The curse of sin and death would be broken, as well as the pattern of authoritarian government. Thus, Jesus would restore man to dominion and would usher in through His Church the purest and most effective government.

That was the plan. And on the day the Jews seemingly triumphed over Jesus by persuading Pilate to crucify Him, everything was working according to plan.

~~~

God's Kingdom cannot peacefully coexist with greed, corruption, pride, hypocrisy and diluted spirituality. His government does not sweetly and gingerly appear on the earth, and hope for the best. It forcefully collides with and exposes man's wrong motives and illegitimate practices; and it serves them a "cease and desist order" from heaven's court.

Jesus hand-delivered that order to Israel's ruling elite; and with it He released God's blueprint for the establishment of His Church, as well as nations and kingdoms. Jesus' presence and ministry served notice to principalities, powers and the people in their grip that God's government was at hand to topple the ungodly systems self-serving men had erected, especially within God's house.

The Pharisees, Sadducees, elders, priests and scribes were entrenched in a religious system, which, over centuries, had increasingly drifted away from the heart of God. Traditions of men prevailed over Jehovah's ways. The Law of Moses, though heeded and upheld, was used as a means to control the people and keep them in subjection. Accusation and condemnation overtook forgiveness and mercy. Religiosity and legalism replaced intimate relationship with God and fellowship with one another.

The religious elite had erected an empire of wealth and prestige at the expense of the poor and uneducated masses. They leveraged fear, particularly the fear of man, to push their agendas. Their hearts were cold. Love was absent. They lived double lives, appearing righteous before their (reluctant) followers, while cultivating godlessness within. They neither led the people; nor did they inspire them. They forcefully upheld a religious system, which had a form of godliness but lacked integrity, authority, power and most importantly, love.

> *They profess to know God, but in works they deny Him, being abominable, disobedient, and disqualified for every good work.* Titus 1:16

John the Baptist had warned Israel's religious leaders, while preaching by the Jordan River, "Repent, for the kingdom of heaven is at hand...flee from the wrath to come...bear fruits worthy of repentance." (Matthew 3:2, 7-8)

> *But the Pharisees and scribes rejected the will of God for themselves...* Luke 7:30

Not only did they ignore John's admonitions, they soon raised their voices and hands against the One, whose way John had been assigned to prepare.

They did not act merely out of jealousy for Jesus' spiritual gifts or His phenomenal appeal with the crowds. The source of their defiance was a satanically-inspired and politically-driven abhorrence for the government of God.

With minor exceptions, as in the case of Nicodemus, the Pharisees, Sadducees, scribes, priests, and elders did not want the Kingdom of God in any measure. They preferred their special privileges over humbly serving the people; intimidation over compassion; schemes over truth; hypocrisy over sincerity; control over freedom; partiality over justice; and ultimately, Caesar and Rome over Jesus and God's Kingdom.

"We have no king but Caesar." John 19:15

~~~

Government Collision is written to share truth and understanding about the nature and functioning of God's government, primarily in and through Christ's Church. The Church is not presented here as an organization, but an organism — a body comprised of numerous members. Each member has a unique design and destiny. In order to maximize his/her personal potential and contribute towards the body's collective mandate for dominion, every individual has to cooperate and co-labor with the other members. The entire body then must be in alignment with and operate by the principles that govern the heavenly Kingdom they've been appointed to establish on earth.

The story of Jesus, particularly the clash between His Kingdom and the religious/political systems of His day, will serve as the backdrop and foundation for each chapter. We start from the beginning — Bethlehem-- and gradually learn our way through various portions of Jesus' life, in which the government of God and its collision with alternate forms of rule is illustrated.

The hellish conspiracy to eliminate Jesus is the thread running throughout the book, culminating with His execution on Calvary. Christ's crucifixion, though the product of a sinister plot by evil men, was also in accordance with the master plan of our loving God. Jesus' death satisfied hell momentarily, but it unleashed heaven eternally. His enemies did not shut down His Kingdom operation. Three days after His death, Jesus walked through a vault into a garden, and then through walls into a room, saying, "I am He who was dead, but is alive forever more. And he who believes in Me will never die!"

We, His Church, are they who believe in Him. We are the carriers of God's government and peace. Jesus has granted to us through declaration by the Holy Spirit, all the "things that the Father has" (John 16:15). We have access to all divine gifts, tools and attributes. Our assignment is the same as Jesus': Release the Kingdom of God and establish dominion over everything He created.

The task is not easy, for reformation always stirs up opposition. Yet, our goal is feasible, because it is backed by God's authority and love. May He increase and abound in us as we further explore the realms of God's government together. And may the Kingdom our Father has bestowed to "the Son of His love" (Colossians 1:13); may *His* Kingdom come and His will be done, on earth as it is in heaven!

Read on!

CHAPTER 1:

ALL ABOUT JESUS

Operating by the standards and principles of God's Kingdom and government must stem from and be dependent upon a vibrant relationship with Jesus Christ, as Savior and Lord.

The Bible clearly points out the most fundamental elements by which God governs His Kingdom:

Righteousness and justice are the foundation of Your throne; Mercy and truth go before Your face. Psalm 89:14.

Righteousness, justice, mercy and truth are founded on the two most prevalent attributes of God's nature: His holiness and love. Righteousness and truth come from God's holiness; mercy and justice from His goodness and love.

It is important to keep these core components of Kingdom government in mind throughout our journey in this book.

The government of God is not merely an administrative system, originating from God's mind and enforced by His hand. It stems from His heart, and it is a reflection of His nature. All the structures and principles within the Kingdom flow out of the heart of God. *We* come from His heart as well!

God founded His Kingdom on love and holiness. Jesus, His Son, modeled, framed and brought forth Kingdom government on the earth, not to expose man's wrongdoing, without revealing and making available the remedy; not to control and subjugate, but to free and empower. Jesus did not come to humiliate people and keep them in check; rather, through His example and sacrifice, to save them from sin and release them into their God-given destiny.

At the time of Jesus, the ecclesiastical and political government of Israel only condemned sin. Jesus never overlooked or covered up sin; however, while exposing people's weaknesses and shortcomings, Jesus was also brokering mankind's freedom from sin's bondage. This premise is illustrated through an incident recorded in the eighth chapter of John's gospel:

The scribes and Pharisees brought to Jesus a woman who had been caught in the act of adultery. They set her in the middle of a crowd and accused her before Him.

> *Now Moses in the law, commanded us that such should be stoned. But what do You say?* John 8:5

The Pharisees and scribes leveraged the Law of Moses for two reasons:

1) Authority to condemn the woman.
2) Opportunity to test Jesus, "that they might have something of which to accuse Him." (John 8:6)

After being pressed for an answer, Jesus, who had initially ignored the accusers, spoke and said the person who was without sin should throw the first stone at the adulteress. From the oldest to the youngest, the Pharisees and scribes "went out one by one." Then Jesus turned to the woman and asked:

> *Where are those accusers of yours? Has no one condemned you?*

> *No one, Lord.*

Neither do I condemn you. Go and sin no more.
John 8:10-11

The Pharisees and scribes wanted to use their govern-mental authority and influence with the people to condemn the woman. Jesus used *His* to forgive her and to inspire her to forsake the sinful lifestyle.

The fear of sin's consequences is a deficient motivator for a high standard of purity and integrity in our lives. Our desire to walk uprightly in our homes, churches, businesses, schools, etc. must stem, primarily, from a passion to honor God and a desire to reap temporal and eternal rewards for righteousness and obedience. An effective pursuit of holiness stems from the peace and joy from being pure, more so than the fear of sin's after-effects.

I don't believe the adulteress ever fell into the same sin. Through her encounter with Jesus Christ, she was instantly aligned with God's government and empowered to walk out her salvation.

Jesus came, not just to demonstrate divine love, but to personify it. He didn't only operate with love; He became love to all people, especially to the most hardened of sinners. Hundreds of years before His arrival, the psalmist David said, "Good and upright is the Lord; therefore He teaches sinners in the way." (Psalm 25:8). So true!

God's love for mankind is the unmatched, revolutionary element in God's government. If we believe that God is love, then "government of God" should also read, "government of Love." The chief reason why the adulteress and a score of other sinners--the woman at the well (John 4), Zaccheus (Luke 16), Mary Magdalene (Luke 8), and you and I--stopped living in sin is because of our encounter with Love through Jesus Christ.

~~~

In a subsequent chapter, we will examine more closely the manner in which Jesus' enemies frequently challenged His authority, and tried to assert theirs by posing tricky questions. For now, we turn our focus on one such interaction with a stunning outcome. We begin at the end of the story:

> *Now when Jesus saw that he answered wisely, He said to him, "You are not far from the kingdom of God." But after that no one dared question Him.*
> Mark 12:34

In this particular moment, Jesus' response to a question posed by a scribe rendered the inquirer and all other religious leaders, who were listening in, unable to question Jesus about *anything* from that day on. In other words, Jesus' answer was the final blow to his critics' use of doctrine, tradition, reason, or legalities to ambush Him.

Why? How did this particular encounter bring about such a formidable shutdown of His enemies' ask-n-trap tactics?

First, we must understand the setting. The scribe's question was not an isolated query, but part of a multi-faceted assault by the Jewish rulers against Christ's credibility and authority. It started with the chief priests, scribes and elders. Earlier that day, they had questioned the source of Jesus' authority "to do these things." (Mark 11:28) That had gotten them in trouble, because Jesus responded with a question they couldn't answer, and then proceeded to speak a parable against them. We will look at that interaction in more detail in a later chapter.

Once the chief priests, et al. were caught in their own trap, "they left Him and went away." Still being bent on exposing Jesus, however, they dispatched another detail, comprised of Pharisees and Herodians. Their tactic remained the same: Ask questions "to catch Him in His words." (Mark 12:13)

The new inquisitors asked Jesus about taxes. "Is it lawful to pay taxes to Caesar?" He answered brilliantly: "Give Caesar what belongs to him and give God what belongs to Him."

The Sadducees joined in next, with their own trying questions. Once again, Jesus rose to the occasion with a superb response and a strong rebuke. The ambush was falling apart. *This* Man could not be lured into any self-incriminating statements, whatsoever!

It was at that point the scribe made his move. He had "heard them reasoning together" and recognized that Jesus "had answered them well."

The scribe asked:

Which is the first commandment of all? Mark 12:28

In other words, "I heard all the things You've been talking about. Tell me, what's the most important directive from God? What's the bottom line here?"

The scribe may have tried to come across as a genuine seeker, but he posed a probing question within an atmosphere that was already saturated with tension. In doing so, the scribe set himself and his colleagues up for a spiritual knock-out punch from Jesus.

There is nothing wrong with questions, as long as those who ask are desirous to learn, or even just curious. Questions such as the ones the religious leaders asked Jesus always had strings attached, connecting them to the inquirers' judgmental, critical spirits and their devious agendas.

The moment someone says, "I have a question for you," we should prayerfully activate our discernment to determine the condition of the person's heart and his/her motive for asking. Our leadership team has often found the following scenarios to be loaded with tell-tale signs of insincerity:

- When someone asks a question for which he/she already knows the answer. The reason for asking is not to learn, but either to see how we respond or to influence others who may be present. The Jewish leaders were masters at this.
- "Small" questions by which the inquirer tries to set us up for a "big" question. In an environment of trust and honor, one should get to the point right away. No need for setups.
- When people ask questions to change the subject. Honest communication should be devoid of misdirection.
- When someone asks a hard or deep question they know we cannot or would not readily answer. E.g. "Do you know the chemical properties of each of the precious stones mentioned in the book of Revelation?" The motive behind such questions is usually the inquirer's desire to answer it for us, thus giving us a piece of their mind.

- Questions posed with the intent to put the inquirer in a position of control. E.g., "How would you feel if I told you there was 'sin in the camp', and I knew exactly where it's coming from?" [I can't resist—my answer would be: "I would feel you're out of order in approaching me about it this way."]

With wisdom, authority, poise, and just a few well-placed words, leaders can expose and overturn insincerity, and prevent it from spreading. The key is to be confident in our identity, exercising the full measure of our authority in every situation. Jesus always operated, first and foremost, as God's beloved Son; a Son in constant communion with the Father. He was also fully aware that His spiritual authority trumped all the ploys of antagonistic Jewish leaders.

Little did the scribe know that when he asked the Lord his "bottom-line" question, he and his cronies would be served with the ultimate bottom-line answer.

"The first commandment," Jesus replied, was to love God "with all your heart, with all your soul, with all your mind, and with all your strength." He then added the second commandment—"You shall love your neighbor as yourself." (Mark 12:30-31)

The scribe acknowledged Jesus' right response, and went on to reiterate and expound on the subject. It was a textbook example of, "Good job—but now look what I can add to what you said":

Well said, Teacher…you have spoken the truth…there is one God, and there is no other but He…and to love

Him...and to love one's neighbor as oneself, is more than the whole burnt offerings and sacrifices.
Mark 12:32, 33

Jesus noted the scribe's insight—that love for God and people was more important than sacrifices. It was a good point. The scribe had definitely done better than all the other members of the devious delegation. Then, Jesus showed him the bottom line:

You are not far from the Kingdom of God.

In other words, "You're not in the Kingdom."

"Your basic doctrine is correct; you have better understanding than your colleagues; you are close, but not there yet."

No more questions. Not on that day; not on any day.

They had pushed too hard; they had gone too far; and now they were paying for it. I can see the Pharisees, Herodians, Sadducees, and scribes walking away, one after another. There wasn't much talking; perhaps some muttering here and there. The scribe walked slowly, pondering what had just happened.

"Not far from the Kingdom? *Me*? I've served God all my life. I know the Scriptures. I speak in the synagogue. I had a good point back there. What do you mean, I'm not far from the Kingdom?!"

The blow did not come just from the words Jesus spoke, but from the authority backing them. He wasn't the upstart from Nazareth His enemies perceived Him to be. And He was never, not for one moment, on the defensive. When Jesus judged the thoughts and intents of his critic's heart, He spoke with authority as the King of God's Kingdom and the Door through which all who truly desire God must enter.

The scribe saw the Door and, in a sense, agreed the Door was positioned right; yet, he did not walk in. The scribe agreed with Jesus doctrinally, and even affirmed the Lord with kind words, but he did not open his heart to believe in Him and surrender to His lordship.

At the end of the encounter, Israel's rulers knew they had no more questions to ask. They had reached the end of that particular road, and only two paths lay before them: Surrender to Him or Eliminate Him.

We all know the path they took.

~~~

My wife, Danielle, and I were appointed as pastors of Valley Shore in 2005. It was an existing work in need of revitalization. On our first Sunday, we had twenty-four people in attendance.

During our first year as leaders, I observed the same pre-service ritual every Sunday. I drove to a spot in town where I could get a good view of the ocean. Then I prayed, bringing the same request before God every week: "Lord, please draw people and resources to our church. Help us to win many souls, and to grow."

God did bring people to us. Some had left other churches; some were new followers of Christ. Little by little, the church grew. God was certainly answering our prayers. But I knew there was more, so I kept going to the same spot and praying the same way every Sunday.

After one year, God spoke to my heart. He told me to stop asking Him for people and resources, but to ask that He would give us wisdom and strength to establish His government in our ministry. God said when His government was in place, *He* would come to our church; consequently, everything else needed for growth and expansion would be drawn to us as well. He also told me to stop my little Sunday ritual.

I did not know what establishing His government meant or entailed; and I certainly had no idea what it would cost. Yet, we obeyed what God said and trusted Him to show us His ways. Step by step, the Lord has been teaching us. We have been through many processes, with varying results. We have had some great successes, and we have suffered some huge losses. We have made some good calls, and we have been responsible for some big mistakes.

We have learned this much: God is attracted to His government. He inhabits families, churches, businesses, kingdoms, and nations, which operate according to the principles that govern His Kingdom; then, by His Spirit, He draws all the human and material resources needed to prosper the places where He dwells.

The most central elements of God's government are love and holiness, both of which are fully embodied and perfectly demonstrated by Jesus. When we receive Him into our lives, we are changed by God. His love flows from His heart to govern our lives; and through us, the nations.

Once Jesus is Lord of our hearts, we are also increasingly impacted by God's holiness. We learn to value what He values and to forsake what He forbids. Sinful patterns lose their grip on us. Righteousness is most appealing. By His grace, the Lord cleanses us, purifies us and shows us how to be more like Him each and every day. His love and purity operating through our lives draw favor and support for our endeavors.

God's government does not function to give men or the organizations they lead control over people--to rule over them through lofty principles, policies or laws. The government of God is all about giving authority and power *to* the people who are in right standing—in relationship—with Him.

The key by which we gain access into God's Kingdom and a seat in His government is Jesus Christ. Just as a wise, earthly king delegates responsibility and grants privileges to those who are in good standing with him, so the King of Kings qualifies and deploys His Kingdom's servants on the basis of relationship.

The government of God is first and foremost about surrendering to Jesus as God's Son, Messiah, Lord and King. The world is His. The universe is His. God's Kingdom is His. Everything we are and do within the realm of God's government depends on our relationship with Jesus Christ.

May we continue to grow in Him, even as we turn the remaining pages of this book!

CHAPTER 2:

MORE THAN A PRODIGY

And the Child grew and became strong in spirit, filled with wisdom; and the grace of God was upon Him.

Luke 2:40

The last verse in John's gospel is overwhelming to me. It evokes the same feeling I believe a climber would have under the following circumstances: She completes an arduous ascent to the peak of a very tall mountain, only to discover there is an insurmountable mountain range up ahead; a range that was initially obscured by the mountain she just scaled.

> *And there are also many other things that Jesus did, which if they were written one by one, I suppose that even the world itself could not contain the books that would be written.* John 21:25

Based on John's statement, the four gospels of Matthew, Mark, Luke, and John, as well as the rest of the New Testament, offer limited information about Jesus' life. I liken what we know about the Lord to the tall mountain, and the myriad of unwritten books to the mountain range beyond.

Essentially, the biblical "biography" of Christ is a mere scratch on the tip of an iceberg. For greater revelation and understanding of His nature and ways, we have to rely on our ever-deepening relationship with God and revelation by the Holy Spirit.

Among the myriad of episodes absent from the written record, is information regarding Jesus' childhood, adolescence and young adulthood. The New Testament covers His first thirty years as follows:

- **Matthew**: 29 verses from chapters 1 and 2, with a very sudden shift from the young Jesus living in Nazareth with his parents, to his baptism by John at age thirty.
- **Mark**: No account whatsoever. Mark 1 begins with Jesus' baptism.
- **Luke**: 81 verses (chapters 1-2).
- **John**: No account. John 1 begins with Jesus' baptism as well.

Within four chapters and a total of one hundred and ten verses is everything we know about Jesus, from His birth to the launching of His ministry. And only thirteen of those verses speak of Jesus' life between the time He was dedicated at the temple and His baptism at the Jordan River. (Luke 2:40-52)

Even so, within those thirteen verses is sufficient evidence that Jesus, even at a very young age, was endued with all the necessary qualities to establish and release God's government; and ultimately, to set the pattern for dominion over the whole world.

~~~

When Jesus lived on the earth, God's government rested on Him. As we saw in the Introduction, Isaiah prophesied that "the government shall be upon His shoulders..." The prophet also said, "Of the increase of His government and peace there will be no end." (Isaiah 9:6, 7)

Christ's government and peace are unstoppable and never-ending, because He has placed that same mantle of government that rested on Him, on His followers. God is within everyone who has surrendered to Jesus' lordship; and so is His government. Christ-followers operate within the confines of the government of God to release the Kingdom of God on the earth. Our objective is always the same--to glorify God.

If the government of God was a structure within our being, it would be standing on four main pillars--integrity, authority, wisdom, and favor.

What we know of Jesus' early life indicates the four pillars were already firmly in place, long before He began His ministry. Two verses from Luke's gospel paint the picture:

> *Then He went down with them and came to Nazareth, and was subject to them...And Jesus increased in wisdom and stature, and in favor with God and men.* Luke 2:51-52

Let's examine the four pillars of government in young Jesus Christ:

INTEGRITY

To walk with integrity is to walk honorably and uprightly before God and men. Jesus' interaction with some leaders and his earthly parents during an incident at age twelve indicates that the pillar of integrity was well in place:

Jesus had accompanied Mary and Joseph to Jerusalem for the annual Feast of the Passover. When the days of the Feast had ended, the family began the northward trek home to Nazareth. Unbeknownst to Joseph and Mary, Jesus had stayed back. The couple had assumed Jesus was traveling with other relatives or acquaintances. After a day's journey, most likely at night--when the children meet their parents to sleep as a family unit--it became clear Jesus was not on this trip.

Deeply concerned, as any parent would be, Joseph and Mary returned to Jerusalem to search for their son. After their frantic three-day search throughout the city, Jesus' parents finally found Him in the temple. He had been there the whole time, "sitting in the midst of the teachers, both listening to them and asking them questions." (Luke 2:46) Jesus' presence, demeanor and words bewildered those who were gathered; and His parents were amazed as well.

Undoubtedly relieved, but still shaken, Mary asked, "Son, why have you done this to us? Your father and I have sought you anxiously." (Luke 2:48)

Three facts in the next three verses of the text provide evidence for the pillar of integrity:

1) Jesus wondered why they sought Him. "Did you not know that I must be about My Father's business?" (vs. 49)
2) Mary and Joseph did not understand what Jesus meant. (vs. 50)
3) Jesus returned to Nazareth with them, "and was subjected to them." (vs. 51)

Jesus clearly knew His identity as God's Son at the age of twelve. He also knew His responsibility to "be about [His] Father's business." His staying back in Jerusalem after the Feast was due to the fact Jesus was walking in His identity and assignment. And, by all indication, He was already bearing fruit:

All who heard Him were astonished at His under-standing and answers. Luke 2:47

Jesus' parents had recognized He was God's Son all along; however, they did not fully understand Jesus' calling. They did not even think to look in the temple first, but spent three days combing other parts of the city. They did not understand why their son stayed back in Jerusalem to hang out at the temple, without even letting them know. They expressed their concern and headed back to Nazareth.

Jesus knew He wasn't carrying Joseph's physiological DNA. He also knew that God's initiatives in His heart, such as spending three days in the temple, superseded the expectations and operations of all people, including Mary and Joseph. Even so, Jesus submitted to Mary and Joseph. He returned with them and yielded to their authority for as long as He lived under their roof.

The pillar of integrity in Jesus is seen in that He honored Mary and Joseph, while knowing God was His true Father. He submitted to their authority, while being fully aware of His divine authority. Moreover, Jesus listened to teachers in the temple and asked questions when, evidently, He possessed superior knowledge and understanding. Jesus certainly walked honorably and uprightly before all people. The pillar of integrity was solid.

AUTHORITY

We examine authority within God's government more extensively in the next chapter; therefore, our discussion of this particular pillar will be very brief.

It is not accidental that Luke's statement of Jesus increasing in wisdom, stature and favor (2:52) follows the account of His submission to His earthly parents (2:51). In the Kingdom of God, obtaining divine authority is contingent upon submitting to earthly authority. Because Jesus honored the authority of His earthly parents and other leaders, God granted Him ever-increasing authority for His assignment.

As we will see below, an unprecedented and unlimited measure of authority manifested immediately upon the start of Jesus' earthly ministry. His empowerment stemmed from His continual increase in stature — significance and ability — throughout His younger years; and that increase was the result of Christ's submission to God and man's authority.

It is very important for parents, teachers, coaches and all other authority figures to teach younger generations to honor authority. Schools, in particular, must make "honor training" a priority. Students, who lack aptitude to successfully pursue any given subject, sport or career, may simply switch to something else. If they lack respect for authority, however, they will eventually come to a grinding stop, no matter what they try to accomplish.

During my days in Green Beret boot camp on the island of Cyprus, we were taught the chain of command and proper protocols regarding our interaction with our superiors before we learned how to march, rappel, or shoot a rifle. Every facet of our military service and all the stages of our development as soldiers hinged on our understanding of and submission to the Army's established authority structures.

WISDOM

The episode of Jesus' four days at the temple in Jerusalem after Passover demonstrates the pillar of wisdom on several counts:

1) The temple, as a place where teachers and church leaders shared their knowledge, was more appealing to Jesus than any other place in Jerusalem; hence His choice to spend four days there.
2) Jesus had a desire to associate with men older than Him. (I doubt I would have done likewise, if I had stayed back during a trip to a big city, when I was twelve).
3) Jesus listened to the teachers. Wisdom is not only recognized by what we say, but also by what we listen to. Being quick to listen and slow to speak is a sign of wisdom.

   Listen to counsel and receive instruction, that you may be wise in your latter days. Proverbs 19:20

4) Jesus asked questions. Many times, wisdom is more evident by what a person asks, rather than what he/she responds to.
5) Jesus gave answers and demonstrated understanding, which was astonishing to those who heard Him.
6) He obeyed His parents and returned home with them.
7) He obeyed His heavenly Father by being about His business.

Kings, rulers, princes, nobles and judges all reign and decree justice by wisdom. It is a pillar for government and dominion.

About twenty years after His encounter with the teachers in the temple, Jesus taught in the synagogue at Nazareth. And just like He did in Jerusalem at age twelve, the Lord astonished those who heard Him. They exclaimed:

> *Where did this Man get these things? And what wisdom is this which is given to Him, that such mighty works are performed by His hands!* Mark 6:2

Jesus' countrymen did not receive Jesus. They failed to perceive Him for who He was, as Messiah and Lord. They could only relate to Jesus as "the carpenter, the Son of Mary, and brother of James, Joses, Judas, and Simon;" therefore, "they were offended at Him." (vs. 3) Even so, the people of Nazareth who heard Jesus at the synagogue made a very accurate observation: His amazing teaching and His miraculous works stemmed from wisdom.

FAVOR

Favor is a pillar in God's government because it is a door-opener. The teachers at the temple allowed Jesus to sit among them because He found favor with them. Think about any twelve-year-old you know, and imagine that young boy or girl consorting with the leaders of any particular field — and astonishing them!

As the Lord continued to interact with these leaders, His favor with them increased. Jesus increased in favor with both God and man. Both are necessary for maximum Kingdom impact.

Favor with God grants us access into His heart and ways; it positions us in heavenly realms saturated with God's light and love and filled with understanding and revelation. Favor with God takes us deeper into relationship. Out of our communion with Him comes everything necessary to accomplish our objectives and fulfill our destiny.

Favor with God also establishes us as co-laborers with Him, instead of mere workers on His "payroll."

During my time in college, I worked for two men who dealt in high-end antiques and collectables. The men were wealthy, well-educated, refined, and highly-regarded in social circles. They were accomplished businessmen, who knew their field well and always demonstrated excellence in all their dealings.

The antique dealers owned four acres right on the Delaware River in Pennsylvania, less than a mile from the location where George Washington crossed that river during the Revolutionary War. It was a gorgeous and valuable plot of land, in the middle of which stood a stunning house, full of rare antiques, works of art, musical instruments, and peculiar collectibles from numerous nations.

The men hired me during my freshman year to help maintain their property. Initially, my assignment entailed mowing the yard and weeding in the summer; raking leaves in the fall; trimming hedges and planting flowers in the spring. In the winter, I worked inside the house, painting or staining furniture, reconditioning items for my employers' store, and polishing their copper stove and extensive collection of silver and copper dishware.

I was both paid and treated very well. I worked for these men throughout my undergraduate years and during my first year of graduate school. My bosses appreciated my work ethic and approved of my output. They also noticed I had a desire to understand the commerce involved in their antique business. Little by little, the two men opened up more and more of their antique-dealing world to me. They let me into their thought processes involved with buying and selling certain items. They taught me some of the dynamics involved in negotiations, agreements, contracts, auctions, and more. By the time I finished my studies and parted ways with my employers, I had come to learn many of the inner workings of the antique-collecting trade.

As I grew in favor with them, we grew in relationship; and through relationship, I obtained valuable knowledge and understanding. During my last summer working for the men, they involved me in many of their conversations pertaining to their profitable antique business on the island of Nantucket, Massachusetts.

I attribute much of my passion for and success with trading marbles, toys and other antiques to my association with my employers, who did not treat me as a hired hand, but a co-laborer in their field of expertise. Favor with God does just that—it brings us into His inner courts and into His throne room, where we interact closely and intimately, co-laboring together in the advancement of His Kingdom. God's favor on our lives, and every spiritual and material blessing associated with it, in turn increases our favor with man.

When I began to deal in vintage marbles, I applied many of the principles I had learned from my time with my employers to establish strong relationships with dealers and collectors, and thus a lucrative, enjoyable business-hobby. Favor with my bosses resulted in favor with future buyers and sellers. Likewise, favor with God is the door-opener for good rapport and increased influence with man.

Favor with God and man is not a "fixed asset" in our lives. It can grow over time. The Scriptures indicate that Jesus "increased" in favor, continually. We can, too!

When Solomon admonished his son through the proverbs, he gave special emphasis to two ideals:

> Let not mercy and truth forsake you; bind them around your neck, write them on the tablet of your heart. Proverbs 3:3

The next verse reveals a connection between mercy and truth, and the increase of favor.

> And so find favor and high esteem in the sight of God and man. Proverbs 3:4

As discussed earlier, at the very core of God's government is love and righteousness. Mercy and truth stem from those two most prevalent attributes of God's heart. Mercy is a manifestation of His love; and truth is integral to holiness.

The two chief reasons why Jesus came to the earth were truth and mercy. He preached truth—the gospel of the Kingdom--and showed God's mercy by saving us from our sins. Mercy and truth were the chief motivating forces within Jesus at every stage of His development; hence, His continual growth in favor with God and man.

As our desire and capacity for mercy and truth increases, so will God's favor in our lives.

~~~

Famous young prodigies and renowned teen sensations in the entertainment industry pale in comparison to the twelve-year-old, Jesus Christ. Within the context of the only biblical glimpse into Jesus' early life, we encounter the brilliant, charismatic, anointed, teachable, knowledgeable, engaging, humble and fearless Son of God.

He carried ever-increasing integrity, authority, wisdom, and favor—central pillars of Kingdom government, which would continue to grow and solidify within Him for the next eighteen years; until the Messiah was fully developed and perfectly-positioned for the launch of His explosive, world-changing ministry.

CHAPTER 3:

INSTANT CREDIBILITY

This beginning of signs Jesus did in Cana of Galilee, and manifested His glory; and His disciples believed in Him.

John 2:11

It was a happy day in Cana of Galilee. A wedding! Bride, groom, family, friends, ceremony, reception, a feast. Give or take a few cultural differences, the event resembled wedding celebrations from numerous cultures across the world. The band was playing, people were smiling, food was being served, and the wine was flowing…for a while, that is--then it ran out!

A wedding at Cana without wine would be the equivalent to a factory night shift without caffeine. It couldn't be! Not wine. Fermented or unfermented, red or white, you just don't run out of wine at a Jewish wedding!

We can only imagine the panic among those responsible. The wait staff was scrambling frantically:

"Hey, do you know where there's more wine — my pitcher's out and the barrel's empty!"

"Last I saw there was some over there, but it's gone now."

"Everyone look. There's got to be wine somewhere. And keep this quiet, until we find some!"

"Boss, there is no wine anywhere on the premises. We don't know what happened. No wine."

"We are dead in the water…"

Mary, Jesus and His disciples were guests at *that* wedding. Somehow, upon learning of the wine outage, Mary thought Jesus could do something about the problem. Her impression stemmed from her understanding of Jesus' identity, and three decades of careful observation and deep pondering regarding her son's development.

"They have no wine."

There had to have been a certain "look" accompanying Mary's statement; something that communicated, "I expect You to do something about this."

"Woman, what does your concern have to do with Me? My hour has not yet come." John 2:3, 4

She definitely gave Jesus the look now!

Mary did not accept that response. Hundreds of prophesies about Christ's coming and His wondrous impact on mankind. Then, the angelic announcement, the virgin birth, the shepherds at the manger, the Magi with their gifts, Simeon and Anna at the temple, teaching the teachers at twelve, and thirty years of supernatural upbringing in Mary and Joseph's home. And just when Mary thought the touch of God on His life would become apparent to all—and what better setting than a wedding?—Jesus said His hour hadn't arrived!

She wouldn't have it. Full of faith and determination, and undoubtedly inspired by having raised the Son of God, Mary reached into an invisible realm that can only be accessed by faith, and pulled into that moment what had been reserved for a later time:

> *His mother said to the servants, 'Whatever He says to you, do it.'* John 2:5

We don't know how Jesus processed the interaction, or how long it took before He spoke. But when He *did* speak, something amazing happened.

Jesus told the servants to fill six water pots of stone with water. Each vessel could hold twenty to thirty gallons. Even if some of the pots were partially filled to begin with, Jesus' command involved a very labor-intensive process. They had no faucets with hoses attached; no pumps; no quick way of doing this. At best, servants had to haul water in smaller vessels after drawing it from a well. It was involved and time-consuming work.

Amazingly, they obeyed Jesus. The servants, who were already preoccupied with wedding tasks and the pressing wine-crisis, stopped everything to fill six large stone pots with water!

When Jesus told the wedding staff what to do, He was not known for His ministry of signs or wonders. The turning of water to wine was His *first* miracle. There were no reports of similar breakthroughs through His initiative; no record or reputation preceding Him. Neither had there been any incidents in all of recorded history to validate the use of water to produce wine, instantaneously.

So why did the servants obey the Lord's directive and fill up the pots with water?

The text offers one possibility. Mary told them to do whatever Jesus said. Mary seems to have had a degree of respect and credibility with the servants; perhaps due to her relationship with the host family. The bulk of the answer, however, lies with Jesus Himself:

His command for water came with authority; not Mary's or His, but God's.

~~~

Jesus demonstrated extraordinary authority during His life on earth. When He spoke, it was as if God spoke; and things changed, immediately!

Immediately:

Unsuccessful fishermen were willing to go back out to sea and cast their nets, yet one more time.

The Zebedee brothers opted out of the family fishing business to become His disciples.

A tax collector, Matthew, left his lucrative post to follow Him.

Peter's mother-in-law was healed of fever.

A paralytic picked up his bed and walked.

Demons were cast out.

Withered limbs were restored.

Lepers were cleansed.

Blind eyes opened.

Food multiplied.

Storms abated.

The dead were raised.

In every case, Jesus simply spoke--with authority!

From the very outset of His earthly ministry, crowds of people were greatly astonished by Jesus' words and ways:

> *"He taught them as one having authority, and not as the scribes."* Mark1:22

> *"With authority He command[ed] even the unclean spirits and they obey[ed] Him."* Mark 1:27

> *"His word was with authority..."* Luke 4:32

> *"Even the wind and sea obey[ed] Him!"* Mark 4:41

There can never be government without authority. Authority is power to enforce laws, exact obedience, give commands, make decisions, and judge. Authority is power; delegated power for those responsible to establish order, justice, and a measure of rule in the land.

The authority Jesus exercised throughout His earthly ministry, as well as the authority He later granted His disciples and ultimately His Church, was the supernatural force necessary for the establishing and structuring of God's Kingdom in the world. The moment God's authority manifested through Jesus at the wedding in Cana, the fishing docks by the Sea of

Galilee, Jairus' (dead, then resurrected) daughter's room, or the graveyards of Gadara, the world received notice that God's government was in operation. Right then, Jesus had instant credibility.

~~~

Consider the daughter of a good king; a king who sets a very high standard of morality and integrity. He is an honest and just king; one who is wise, strong, compassionate, and bold.

The princess grows up in her father's courts, being continually surrounded by honorable, honest, and wise leaders and courtiers. Throughout her days as a youth and young adult, she has an insider's perspective on the establishment of laws, the proclamation of decrees, the planning of campaigns, the challenges of administration, the perils of wars, the writing of policy and many other aspects of her father's domain.

The princess' exposure to her father's well-run kingdom equips her with discernment regarding government. Her high-level upbringing and understanding instill high expectations of what a good government should look like and how it should operate. Even the slightest aberration from the standard the princess was raised with, will quickly raise flags.

At the time of Jesus, Israel was like the princess, in that the people had originally come from a good Kingdom. They had been created by a God who loved them. He was their King; and His courts were filled with righteousness and glory. That was Israel's heritage--their spiritual makeup. Over time, men and their traditions established an environment that was much different from God's heart and desire.

When Jesus began His ministry, His exercise of Kingdom authority encouraged and inspired the folks who had been living under the oppressive regime of the existing government—both of Rome and Israel. Immediately, individuals who carried the spiritual DNA of God's righteousness and justice recognized what had been absent and illegitimate in their society all along. People's desire for God and His Kingdom was revived; their faith and hope were reactivated.

Those who know their true identity in Christ can quickly recognize authentic government when they see it. Authority is the first tell-tale. They identify government and perceive its degree of effectiveness according to the manifestation of true Kingdom authority. People can also recognize and (hence) avoid controlling, constricting, manipulative, and oppressive leadership structures.

While Jesus enlightened the masses and established credibility with everyone who partook of His ministry, He infuriated the leaders who were responsible for undermining Kingdom authority through their systems of control.

The demonstration of the gospel of the Kingdom always exposes, confronts, and upsets misbegotten and unlawful religious and political models.

Israel's "authorities" could not match Jesus' authority by their words or deeds; therefore, they tried to use their jurisdiction and clout to challenge Him:

> *Now when He came into the temple, the chief priests and the elders of the people confronted Him as He was teaching, and said, "By what authority are You doing*

these things? And who gave You this authority?"
Matthew 21:23

Jesus responded, not by defending or explaining His authority; instead, He demonstrated it. The Lord asked His critics His own question; one that proved His superior understanding of the subject:

The baptism of John — where was it from? From heaven or from men? Matthew 21:25

The chief priests and elders were stumped. If they said John's baptism was from man, they would have lost (even more) credibility with the crowd—because the people considered John a prophet. If they answered that John was sent from God, Jesus would have confronted them for not receiving John. Caught between Jesus' impeccable logic and their fear of the multitude, the religious leaders admitted not knowing the answer, and backed off.

~~~

Has anyone you have tried to convince about God's love ever questioned you as to why God doesn't stop mass murderers, corrupt leaders, barbarous dictators, terrorists, thieves and warmongers? Or, why He doesn't prevent swarms of locusts and other pests from devouring crops and destroying people's livelihood? Why doesn't God expose and bring to justice spies, conspirators, and traitors before they ply their dark trade and jeopardize entire nations? Why doesn't God intervene more and block evil people and happenings?

I have heard those questions many times; and I have heard the following response often, even from devout Christ-followers: "God doesn't cause evil, but allows it to happen for a reason."

It's a nice-sounding answer, but it is not correct.

God does not allow evil; *we* do! He doesn't intervene, because that's *our* job!

After God created the earth, He made us stewards of it. He gave man the responsibility to care for His creation and to "have dominion over the works of [His] hands." (Psalm 8:6)

> *The heaven, even the heavens are the LORD's, but the*
> *earth He has given to the children of men.*
> Psalm 115:16

With the responsibility, God also granted us authority; not so we can flaunt it through lofty titles in front of our names and engraved plaques on our mailboxes, doors and desks, but to properly administer God's government and peace within the domains of our influence and responsibility.

In one of his letters, Paul exhorts Titus to "set in order the things that [were] lacking" in Crete. (Titus 1:5) He tells Titus to appoint elders in every city, and gives him specific qualifications for that task. Paul admonishes Titus to "speak the things which are proper for sound doctrine"; and thereby, to eradicate idle talk and deception (2:1); to stop those who were subverting "whole households, teaching things which they ought not, for the sake of dishonest gain." (1:10-11).

Paul then outlines the proper standards Titus must nurture in the church, regarding the disposition and behavior of the young and old alike, and of bondservants. (2:2-10) He emphasizes the importance of living "soberly, righteously, and godly" for the sake of "our great God and Savior, Jesus Christ, who gave Himself for us" to make us "his own special people, zealous for good works."(2:12, 14)

Furthermore, Titus was to remind the Cretans "to be subject to rulers and authorities, to obey, to be ready for every good work." They were to speak well of everyone, be gentle, peaceable and humble towards all men. (3:1-2)

Paul commands his son in the faith to affirm those principles continually, "that those who have believed in God should be careful to maintain good works."(3:8)

> *Speak these things, exhort, and rebuke, with all authority.* Titus 2:15

Clearly, Paul expected Titus to exercise his authority as the leader over that particular work in Crete. Paul would gladly pray for his young protégé; he would speak God's grace and mercy and peace over him, and would articulate the Kingdom ideals and standards; however, Paul would not do the job for him-- Titus had to step up and govern.

As a pastor, I cannot expect God or any man to lead my congregation for me. The Lord appointed *me* and gave me authority over this particular area of His government. As I continually lift up the work in prayer, I trust God will grant me wisdom, resources, strength, and support. He will help and encourage me; He will bring correction when needed. God will always give me vision and direction; He will show me His ways and unfold His paths before me; but He will not take over!

God entrusted you and me with the administration of His creation. He made us rulers over the realms of earthly existence He has designed. Jesus delegated responsibility to us and made available to us heavenly power and authority to accomplish our tasks. After we have prayed for His wisdom and grace; and after receiving all the training He has provided during seasons of preparation, we must arise and co-labor with Father, Son and Holy Spirit. No amount of prayer will move God to do what He has entrusted *us* with. What will move Him is our forward motion towards the assignment He gave us.

~~~

One of the most pivotal moments in Jesus' earthly ministry occurred on a stormy night on the Sea of Galilee. Just a few hours earlier, the Lord and His disciples had fed thousands of people, when five loaves and two fish multiplied miraculously. Twelve baskets of food were taken up as leftovers!

Following the feeding of the multitude, Jesus directed His disciples to get into a boat and cross over to the other side of the large lake. While the disciples were in the middle of their journey, "tossed by the waves," Jesus suddenly appeared, walking towards them on the waves.

The disciples were frightened — more by the phenomenon of Jesus walking on water than the choppy sea. The Lord tried to calm them down with His characteristic greeting:

> *Be of good cheer! It is I; do not be afraid.*
> Matthew 14:27

Peter wasn't convinced.

> *Lord, if it is You, command me to come to You on the water.* Vs. 28

Note how Peter was catching onto the authority concept. He recognized that if the man walking on the water was indeed Jesus, a command from Him was all it would take for Peter to do likewise.

Jesus gave the command. Peter walked on water. Then he began to sink. Jesus rescued Peter by stretching out His hand and catching him. What an encounter!

> *And when they got into the boat the wind ceased.*
> Vs. 32

The next verse brings us to the climactic moment:

> *Then those who were in the boat came to Jesus and worshiped Him saying, "Truly, You are the Son of God."* Matthew 14:33

The twelve disciples had witnessed and actively participated in the multiplication of one lad's food to provide for thousands. They had already been with Jesus in Cana, when he had turned water into wine. These men had seen Peter's mother-in-law, all the sick and demoniacs of her town, and scores of other people throughout Galilee miraculously healed and instantly delivered. However, they had not yet recognized and worshiped Jesus as the Son of God--not until they saw Him demonstrating authority and power over creation.

When Jesus walked on the waves and then instantly caused the wind to cease and the sea to calm down, He demonstrated authority over forces that have the capacity to overwhelm men and pull them under. Right then, the disciples became fully convinced He was the Messiah; and they worshiped Him as such!

We are living at a time when God's people must increasingly attract souls to Jesus, by doing the works He did-- "and greater works than these"! (John 14:12) Exercising Christ-like authority over creation will maximize our impact. The world is eagerly searching for a manifestation of genuine, life-transforming, supernatural power. The movie industry, television programming and literature — especially materials with teens as their target audience — are inundated with the concept of humans obtaining and utilizing supernatural power.

Even the wildest scenarios presented on the big screen or in fiction novels pale in comparison to the amazing feats God's children will perform. The realm of having dominion over creation is one Jesus demonstrated and paved the way for us to enter into. I am fully confident that in the days ahead, the Church will take up that mantle and glorify God by the most amazing demonstrations of power and authority over creation, ever!

CHAPTER 4:

SHAKE-UPS AND CONFRONTATIONS

"But when the chief priests and scribes saw the wonderful things that He did, and the children crying out in the temple and saying, 'Hosanna to the Son of David!' they were indignant..."

Matthew 21:15

An international interfaith conference concluded that more than one hundred thousand Christians are martyred annually. On average, a Christian is killed for his/her faith every five minutes. The number does not include civil wars or wars between nations.[1] In many nations, churches are not allowed to own property, and Christians face many forms of discrimination and abuse continually.

Governments don't oppress Christians, and militants don't turn into murderers of peaceful worshipers just because of differing beliefs. The problem is not what Christ-followers *believe*, but what has been deposited in them from the One in whom they put their faith.

Every genuine follower of Jesus carries the revelation, authority, anointing, favor and power to bring reformation and truth to every realm of society. When a believer walks in submission and obedience to God, applying the principles by which His Kingdom operates, God's government begins to flow out of that individual, setting the stage for dominion. The spiritual, socio-economic and political landscapes start to shift.

---

[1] "Shocking Figures Reveal 105,000 Christians are Martyred Every Year." Daniel Blake, *The Christian Post,* June 8, 2011

The Bible states, and numerous reports from around the world confirm, that even the physical earth is healed and becomes fruitful in response to "the revealing of the sons of God." (Romans 8:19)

When God rises up in His people and God's people arise to their rightful places of authority, governments collide. Counterfeit dominion is exposed and perpetrators are warned: "Time's up. Repent; reform!"

~~~

The amazing results that attracted crowds to Jesus' gatherings also attracted criticism and opposition. The two often went hand in hand. Jesus would speak or pray for the sick in villages, cities, or the countryside. People would flock to Him from every direction. They "laid the sick in the market-places," hoping Jesus would minister to them. Some even "begged Him that they might just touch the hem of His garment."

> *And as many as touched Him were made well.*
> Mark 6:56

The religious elite never celebrated or even noted the amazing breakthroughs. On the contrary:

> *Then the Pharisees and some of the scribes came together to Him...When[a] they saw some of His disciples eat bread with defiled, that is, with unwashed hands, they found fault.* Mark 7:1-2

People with a critical, judgmental spirit are not moved by insightful teachings or by signs, wonders and miracles. If they are present when such things happen, the most we can hope for is a cease-fire; rarely, if ever, a surrender. Even the most profound revelation and greatest demonstrations of super-natural power will not impact prideful, self-righteous, cynical hearts.

Repeatedly, Jesus would phenomenally move in Kingdom power and authority, dramatically transforming people's bro-ken lives. However, just as in the episode above, the Pharisees and their cronies would raise an issue about something minute and irrelevant, clearly indicating their eyes and hearts were never focused on what God was doing. Their agenda of discrediting Jesus always took preeminence over the Father's expressions of love and power.

The behavior of Israel's religious leaders towards Jesus is not much different than the resistance that moves of God encounter today. The manifestation of God's might and glory within a realm where God's government is established often draws similar reproach or even attack.

Below are examples of such opposition. Unfortunately, we have experienced all of them throughout our journey to know God more intimately and release His Kingdom through our lives and labors. I include them, not to share battle stories; nor to draw sympathy. I present them as symptoms of a (spiritual) heart condition which must be diagnosed and remedied in the body of Christ:

- *Questioning the authenticity of miracles and Spirit manifestations.* I have yet to meet a critic, whose first thoughts or words when someone shares an emo-tional testimony of an instantaneous healing are, "I'm so happy for her!" Instead, we hear, "We'll see about that." We certainly acknowledge that healings should be verified by members of the medical community; yet, why can't we rejoice with those who rejoice until the verification comes?

- *Accusations against leaders of revivals.* Even in a scenario where a move of God is poorly led, accusation will never make things better. If there are errors in doctrine or practice, or if the move lacks sound leadership, we need God's intervention. Accusation does not attract God to the situation. He is not drawn to what He doesn't spawn.

- *Emphasizing how "these things" do not line up with established doctrine and existing beliefs.* I'm amazed by individuals who speak against ministries on the internet or from pulpits, citing "unbiblical teachings and practices." Where in the Bible are we admonished to publically criticize individuals and their work, without at least trying to speak with them first?

- *Rallying support against a movement, by broadcasting negative statements.* We never preoccupy ourselves with responses to accusations and rumors. We are fully confident that over time, the fruit will speak for itself. Some of my most rewarding moments in ministry come when I meet with city leaders, members of our local business community, or highly-educated folks, who say: "You and your church are the farthest thing from what people have told me. I want to attend some of your meetings."

- *Demonstrations of anger and rage.* I was once manhandled during a healing service by a lady who felt the music was too loud. Obviously, there was a deeper issue involved.

- *Scheming and maneuvering to put an end to what is taking place.* This is dangerous—for the assailants. I do not know of even one case in all of church history, in which individuals who took on the task of maligning or shutting down a move of God, ended well. Unless they repent, the perpetrators will continue down a path which does not lead anywhere good.

The root cause of such attitudes and behavior boils down to the absence of genuine, unconditional love. God is love. That means God and love are one and the same. If we want to find God, we look for love. At some point in their spiritual journey, critics of moves of God lost the tenderness and wonder God's love evokes.

On one occasion, Jesus confronted the religious rulers with the following rebuke:

> *Even so, you also outwardly appear righteous to men,*
> *but inside you are full of hypocrisy and lawlessness.*
> Matthew 23:27-28

I find the Lord's reference to them as "lawless" very interesting. Here were men of God, whose government, theology and practice were centered, primarily, on the Law of Moses. They were teachers and administrators of the Law. They offered sacrifices, held prayer services, and established numerous traditions, including wearing phylacteries—leather pouches containing scrolls of parchments with portions of the Law. God's Law seemed to be very important to the leaders of Israel; yet, Jesus called them law*less* hypocrites!

The Lord wasn't impressed with repetitive prayers, fancy robes, big titles, long teachings, and man-made traditions. Being law-abiding is a condition of the heart, not an outward expression; and Jesus knew the hearts of the religious rulers were lacking. Over time, they had traded intimate relationship and insatiable passion for God's presence for a superficial adherence to the Law. Their love for God was neither found, nor expressed in wholehearted devotion; rather through their militant enforcement of endless lists of do's and don'ts. Consequently, both the leaders and many of their constituents lacked the most important element of a walk with God, love:

"And because lawlessness will abound, the love of many will grow cold." Matthew 24:12

God's government is established on a foundation of His love, the key characteristics of which are clearly laid out by the Apostle Paul in his first letter to the Corinthian church.

Love:

- Suffers long
- Is kind
- Does not envy
- Does not parade itself
- Is not puffed up
- Does not behave rudely
- Does not seek its own
- Is not provoked
- Thinks no evil
- Does not rejoice in iniquity
- Rejoices in the truth
- Bears all things
- Believes all things

- Hopes all things
- Endures all things

All four gospels show Jesus' enemies operating by the exact opposite standard. Nothing they spoke or did against Jesus in the name of God, even closely resembled God. They did not know love; they did not know God; therefore they took a strong stand against Jesus.

~~~

The Lord always responded remarkably to all the opposition He faced. He also leveraged confrontations with the religious elite for the benefit of His disciples. Jesus taught valuable lessons by drawing from the frequent episodes of Pharisaical hostility towards Him. One day, while He was ministering to the masses — with great results, as usual--the Pharisees once again, were preoccupied with finding fault.

> *"Why do Your disciples transgress the tradition of the elders? For they do not wash their hands when they eat bread."* Matthew 15:2

Jesus responded with a question of His own:

> *"Why do you also transgress the commandment of God because of your tradition?* (vs. 3)

Christ confronted the Pharisees for demanding obedience regarding practices such as washing hands, while they themselves were living with filth on the inside. He cited lack of honor for their parents as one of the many ways by which they had "made the commandment of God of no effect by [their] tradition." (vs. 7)

Then, with one sentence—a quote from a prophecy by Isaiah--Jesus completely dismantled His critics' sanctimonious behavior:

> *"They draw near Me with their mouth, and honor Me with their lips, but their heart is far from Me."* (vs. 8)

Jesus' next move was pivotal for the eyewitnesses of that debate, and vital for His disciples--and us: He "called the multitude to Himself" and taught them why the Pharisees were wrong to bring up hand-washing:

> *"Not what goes into the mouth defiles a man; but what comes out of the mouth, this defiles a man."* (vs. 11)

Essentially, food being handled with unclean hands would not corrupt a person; but words and actions originating from impure hearts would. Hand-washings and adherence to other rules as such, would never suffice. God only validates cleanliness on the inside.

So true! I wonder how many churches are filled weekly with sharply-dressed, smiling, well-spoken, tithing, serving, rule-keeping men and women who are so quick to criticize or judge leaders and fellow congregants before their cars even leave the parking lot after the service?

Following the Lord's confrontation of His critics, the disciples came to Him, saying His words had offended the Pharisees.

Evidently, the Pharisees voiced their displeasure to the disciples, not to Jesus directly. Such is the behavior of people who are not aligned with the ways of God's government.

Instead of following biblical standards for conflict resolution (Matthew 18:15-17; James 5:20), and communicating directly with leadership, disgruntled folks often try to get to leaders through the "back door," by approaching close confidants or even family members. Whoever operates this way is out of order. If leaders respond by sending word back through the third party their critics involved, they will only magnify the problem.

We must carefully consider the Lord's response to His disciples:

> *"Every plant which My heavenly Father has not planted will be uprooted. Let them alone."*
> Matthew 15:13-14

Jesus commanded the disciples to ignore the scribes and Pharisees. It was not for them to deal with the critics of the move of God. It was *His* responsibility to confront it, and God's prerogative to execute judgment. Jesus would expose them, and unless they repented, God would ultimately uproot them; but the disciples were not to get involved.

Sometimes friends ask how we deal with those who speak or act against us. Our answer is simply, "We don't. We don't deal with them." We bless them, ensure we have a pure heart towards everyone, and turn the matter over to the Lord. We are *His*--members of a Church and soldiers in an army, which belongs to Him. Jesus can deal with our enemies as He wishes; preferably, by touching their hearts with His radical love; through divine encounters that cannot be disputed or dismissed, only desired, for the rest of their days.

The Apostle Paul gives his spiritual son, Timothy, a precious admonition:

> *Avoid foolish and ignorant disputes, knowing that they generate strife. And a servant of the Lord must not quarrel but be gentle to all, able to teach, patient, in humility correcting those who are in opposition, if God perhaps will grant them repentance, so that they may know the truth.* 2 Timothy 2:23-25

On a personal note, Paul's words have carried me through many seasons of reproach and dishonor. These verses inspire me to maintain a high value for peace and joy in my heart, regardless of any sign of contempt around me. I am always aware of the importance of staying encouraged and fervent in my pursuit of God; of following the cloud that directs us to the Promise Land.

In the face of such trials, I withdraw into the secret place and commit the matter to the Lord, who knows the whole truth. I purify my heart before Him, and seek His affirmation and direction. I try to stay in God's presence until He enables me to block out all the adverse effects of reproach; then, I continue the journey, following the cloud and in tune with God's heartbeat.

I have always drawn hope and strength from the following portion of Scripture. May it bless you as well:

> *Let my vindication come from Your presence*
> Psalm 17:2

~~~

Mark's gospel indicates that the Pharisees' resistance against Jesus began just shortly after He began public ministry.

They considered His forgiving of a paralytic's sins blasphemous (Mark 2:7). Next, they questioned His disciples about the company Jesus kept:

"How is it He eats and drinks with tax collectors and sinners?" Mark 2:16

Then, the Pharisees faulted Jesus for some of His disciples' actions. Why did His disciples not fast like John and the Pharisees' disciples? (2:18); and why were they plucking heads of grain from the fields on the Sabbath?

When Jesus entered the synagogue, the Pharisees "watched Him closely" to see whether He would perform healings on the Sabbath, "so they might accuse Him."(3:2)

Jesus looked at them angrily and was "grieved by the hardness of their hearts"; yet, He moved ahead with His agenda. He commanded a man with a withered hand to stretch it out. The hand was instantly restored!

Then the Pharisees went out and immediately plotted with the Herodians against Him, how they might destroy Him. Mark 3:7

Immediately following that healing in the synagogue, a partnership was formed between religious and political leaders to eliminate Jesus. We will look at that partnership in more detail up ahead. For now, we take note of Jesus' response to that early wave of opposition and the subsequent plot.

He ignored it. Jesus was neither affected by the Pharisees' reproach, nor limited by their plotting. He "withdrew with His disciples...and a great multitude from Galilee followed Him..." While the rulers schemed, Jesus poured His life into twelve men, eleven of whom would change the world. Moreover, "a great multitude" from numerous regions in and around Israel flocked to Jesus, because "they heard how many things He was doing." (Mark 3:7-8)

When faced with reproach and persecution, we would do well to follow Jesus' example. Instead of exerting energy and resources to deal with opposition, let us partner with and share our lives into those who are truly for us to impact the multitudes!

CHAPTER 5:

FEARLESSNESS FEARED

And they sent to Him their disciples with the Herodians, saying, "Teacher, we know that You are true, and teach the way of God in truth; nor do You care about anyone, for You do not regard the person of men.

Matthew 22:15-16

Controlling and manipulative leaders rule over people by the fear of man--a demonic stronghold erected and empowered by fear, pride and unbelief.

Think of the fear of man as a two-faced beast. On one side of the head is a face with an intimidating look; on the other side a look of approval. The former uses fear; the latter employs seduction. The ultimate objective is to cause men and women to put their faith in man, rather than God. As with any sin, people's weaknesses make them more vulnerable to attack. Rejection, insecurity, self-importance, and an inordinate need for affirmation function like bellhops for the fear of man--they open the door to the beast and carry in all its baggage.

The religious and political leaders of Israel used the fear of man to force their manifestos and agendas on the people of Israel. They used intimidation to evoke fear; and flattery to bait people into seeking their approval.

Jesus was completely devoid of the fear of man. Neither intimidation, nor seduction could take Him off course. The Lord modeled and imparted to His followers the most effective countermeasure against the fear of man: An unshakable trust in God.

The fear of man brings a snare,
But whoever trusts in the Lord shall be safe.
Proverbs 29:25

We will learn more about Jesus and His victory against the fear of man below. We now turn our attention to another great victor over the "beast." His name was Nehemiah.

Nehemiah had been commissioned by God to rebuild the wall around the city of Jerusalem. The wall had been destroyed during the invasion of the Chaldeans years earlier. Nehemiah's objective was to complete the task within fifty-two days. The resources for the reconstruction of the wall were provided by the Persian king, whom Nehemiah had served as cup-bearer.

Nehemiah had his orders. He was a visionary and a great leader. He inspired the Jews who were assigned to him to join him in giving the reconstruction project their best and undivided attention. No sooner had Nehemiah and his workforce began rebuilding the walls, when opposition appeared.

Two men, Sanballat the Horonite and Tobiah the Ammonite, "were deeply disturbed" that Nehemiah and his crew had been sent "to seek the well-being of the children of Israel." (Nehemiah 2:10)

At first, the two men mocked the rebuilding of the wall and questioned Nehemiah's authority.

What is this thing you are doing? Will you rebel against the king?" Nehemiah 2:19

Nehemiah did not bite. He knew who he was and where his authority had come from: God via the Persian government.

*The God of heaven Himself will prosper us; therefore
we His servants will arise and build.* Nehemiah 2:20

The work continued. So did the resistance. Sanballat was
"furious and very indignant." He and his fellow cynic Tobiah
mocked the project and the workers, calling them "feeble Jews"
and claiming their wall would not even be strong enough to
bear the weight of a fox. (Nehemiah 3:2, 3)

Nehemiah kept his focus on the assignment. He responded to the reproach by directing his voice to God:

*Hear O our God, for we are despised; turn their
reproach on their own heads.* Nehemiah 3:4

When Sanballat and Tobiah realized their usual tactics of
intimidation and mockery were not working against Nehemiah, they threatened with violence:

*All of them conspired together to come and attack
Jerusalem and create confusion.* Nehemiah 4:8

Nehemiah brilliantly defended his position and assignment. Primarily, He expressed trust in God to fight any battle
that might ensue; but he also properly equipped his co-laborers
with weapons and a good plan.

Half the workforce would be building the wall; the other
half would be prepared to ward off a potential attack. A trum-
pet sound would notify everyone which part of the wall was
being assaulted, so everyone could rally.

The work continued. The attack never came.

Sanballat and Tobiah's next wave of opposition targeted Nehemiah, himself. Sidetracking the leader would negatively affect the project just as much, if not more, than a bloody and costly military engagement. Nehemiah's enemies asked him to attend a meeting "among the villages in the plains…"

I inject here that even many of the wholesome and progressive meetings and committees, to which leaders are invited, can be distractions. We must seek the counsel of the Holy Spirit continually, regarding our involvement in various endeavors, to avoid unnecessary diversions of time, energy and resources.

Nehemiah immediately apprehended the ploy. He sent word back that he was doing "a great work" and did not have the time or desire to meet. His enemies persisted, sending messengers four times with the same request. Nehemiah did not budge.

The "people-are-talking-about-you" tactic was next. Sanballat dispatched a messenger to Nehemiah "with an open letter in his hand." The letter was addressed to Nehemiah. It stated there was a report "among the nations" that Nehemiah and the Jews were planning to rebel against the king. (Nehemiah 6:6)

Nehemiah put down his tool long enough to write, "All these allegations are figments of your own imagination"; then, he went back to work. His discernment of the situation was impeccable.

For they all were trying to make us afraid, saying, "Their hands will be weakened in the work, and it will not be done." Nehemiah 6:9

The conspirators were furious. All their tricks had failed. They only had one more card up their sleeve, "the death-threat".

One of their cronies went to Nehemiah and presented himself as a concerned, well-meaning friend. He notified Nehemiah of an imminent attack against his life, and urged the general contractor to leave the wall and take cover in the house of God (where supposedly the attackers would never look).

There it was—satan's best shot against God's children: "You are going to die. Everything you worked for will be for naught. You will end up with nothing."

I have faced that assault many times. The death-threat comes forcefully at first, but it is powerless against those who have been "crucified with Christ". (Galatians 2:20) The dead are never afraid of dying. Once we have died to ourselves and have been consecrated to God, threats of financial loss and physical harm cannot dissuade us from our task. We put our trust in the Lord for protection, and we continue pursuing God's will and purposes.

I recommend the following stand against the death-threat: Go outside and find a good patch of dirt or sand. Use your foot to draw a line. Stand firmly on one side of the line and say aloud, "I am not moving, no matter what the cost. I may lose everything; I may be hurt; I may be killed. I will not be scared away from my destiny!"

I also propose we read Nehemiah's response to his enemies' run-and-hide advice. His last words to them have always been a huge source of encouragement whenever I have faced the death-threat.

Should such a man as I flee? And who is there such as I who would go into the temple to save his life? I will not go in! Nehemiah 6:11

Nehemiah and his crews persisted. The rebuilding of the wall was completed in fifty-two days. None of the threats materialized. Sanballat and Tobiah never made a move against Nehemiah's life or the wall. They were too afraid.

Whenever the fear of man is not allowed entry, it "bounces" back to its source. Then, it works in reverse—the fear-mongers become afraid of the fear-less!

Bullies rule over "playgrounds" by intimidation, rather than strength. They know fear well, because it lives inside them. Bullies are slaves of their fear. They make agreements with it: Prey on the weak and fear will not torment *them*. Sanballat and Tobiah--and in Jesus' case the Pharisees, scribes and elders--wielded fear to exert their will over people and gain control; primarily, because they were afraid of losing control.

When fearless individuals stand up to bullies, fear has nowhere to go, except where it came from—the bully's heart.

~~~

When the fear of man cannot gain control by intimidation, it turns face. Enter manipulation. The objective is to seduce people into seeking man's approval. Where intimidation wears a frown and operates forcefully, manipulation smiles and proceeds subtly. Consider some examples:

- Flattery—Exploitation of the need for affirmation and recognition. "You are so amazing; and attractive! Your work is exceptional. Everyone thinks very highly of you."

- Gifts—Non-sincere expressions of honor and appreciation attached to strings of performance and obligation. In essence, bribes in disguise, exploiting greed or need.

- Invitations—Exploitation of self-importance and other forms of pride. "We're only inviting a few *special* people. We'd love for you to join us."

- Secrets—Exploitation of a need for inclusion and privilege. "I'm going to entrust you with something very confidential. Don't tell anyone."

Man's approval comes with a price tag; it costs authority. If we succumb to manipulation, we step aside from our God-given position of Kingdom authority. I have often observed this dynamic operating in ministries. Leaders are the primary targets.

In one church, a couple developed a habit of bringing their monetary contributions directly to the pastor, along with personal gifts and kind words. The couple did not place their tithes and offerings in the offering plates during collection times; instead, they held back their offerings until they added up to large amounts. Then, they waited for opportune moments to bring them to the pastor himself.

"Would you please put this in the offering for us? And these (presents) are for you. We love your ministry."

The pastor bit the hook. He received the contributions along with the personal gifts, thus allowing the couple to establish a precedent of circumventing church protocols. Soon, the couple occupied a prominent place in the leader's mind. He was even heard saying, "I love the _____s. They come in from time to time and lay big bucks on me."

One day, the couple's children misbehaved and caused problems during a church-sponsored event. The associate pastor responsible for the event confronted the children and spoke to their parents. Instead of working with the associate to resolve the problem, the couple called the senior pastor directly. Leveraging their (inappropriate) relationship with him, the husband and wife persuaded him to favor their children.

The couple had successfully manipulated the church's senior leader to grant them special privileges at the expense of sound judgment and justice. Ultimately, he had traded authority for the couple's approval and continued support.

The fear of man packs a double punch in such situations. The problem persists (because it is never dealt with properly); and leaders have less authority to deal with it (they lost their authority by compromising personal and organization protocols and standards).

In the event of a fire, no leader would attempt to put it out by trading buckets of water for buckets of gasoline. Yet, trading authority for a few accolades or dollars is doing just that!

~~~

Jesus was never intimidated by men; nor did He ever seek their approval. The fear of man was completely powerless against Jesus, and Israel's religious and political leaders knew it well:

"Teacher, we know that You are true, and teach the way of God in truth; nor do You care about anyone, for You do not regard the person of men." Matthew 22:15-17

Like Nehemiah, Jesus had an assignment from God and a timeframe for its accomplishment. Regardless of the times or seasons of His life, or what swirled around Him—friends or foes; praises or accusations—the Lord kept His focus on the goal and put His trust in His Father. The key was maintaining an accurate sense of identity through relationship.

The words God used while calling the prophet, Jeremiah, to His service illustrate this principle:

"Before I formed you in the womb I knew you; Before you were born I sanctified you; I ordained you a prophet to the nations." Jeremiah 1:5

God "knew" Jeremiah before He created him. In the Hebrew language, the root for this particular use of "know" denotes observation, recognition and care. God observed, recognized and cared for Jeremiah—God was in relationship with him--long before he was born. Within the context of their relationship, God also predetermined Jeremiah's assignment as "a prophet to the nations."

Before God created each of us and gave us a part in the administration of His grace and the advancement of His Kingdom, we had relationship. Everything we are and do must be anchored in that eternal connection.

Jeremiah responded to God's calling by signifying his limitation:

> Ah, Lord God! Behold, I cannot speak, for I am a youth. Vs. 6

God told Jeremiah to stop seeing his age as a hindrance to his destiny. God's grace and calling on Jeremiah's life, and ours, supersedes all human limitations.

Jeremiah was commissioned to go everywhere God would send him, speaking whatever God would command him to share. The next verse is critical:

> Do not be afraid of their faces, for I am with you to deliver you, says the LORD. Vs. 8

God commanded Jeremiah not to allow the fear of man to dissuade him from his task. The commandment came with the assurance of God's presence and protection.

Then, God elaborated on Jeremiah's mission:

> See, I have this day set you over the nations and over the kingdoms, To root out and to pull down, To destroy and to throw down, To build and to plant."
> Vs. 8

Jeremiah's calling was not confined to speaking words from God; *through* God's word he would have authority over nations and kingdoms. He would tear down and build up. He would uproot and plant. God's word over our lives comes with the anointing to transform our environment.

Ultimately, Jeremiah's assignment was to exercise dominion; yet, long before he was given his assignment, Jeremiah had relationship with God. Relationship always comes first; then, the assignment. Dominion flows out of relationship.

God told Jeremiah to "prepare...and arise." Then, He repeated His commandment regarding the fear of man:

> Do not be dismayed before their faces, lest I dismay you before them. Vs. 17

On that day, God established Jeremiah as "a fortified city...an iron pillar and bronze walls against the whole land." The prophet would prevail against "the kings of Judah...its princes...its priests, and against the people of the land." They would fight against him, but they would not prevail.

> "For I am with you," says the Lord, "to deliver you."
> Vs. 18-19

Our mandate for dominion in the earth stems from a relationship which began long before the earth was formed. When we surrender to Jesus and invite Him into our hearts, we experience a true revival—the restoration of a timeless bond with the Living God. The disciplines of prayer, worship, Bible reading, and being in fellowship with other believers help us grow in relationship; however, they do not delineate the confines of our walk with God. Only eternity will fully reveal the full extent of our communion with God before, during and after our earthly years. Only then will we fully understand how much God loves us, not as workers or servants, but as sons.

~~~

Satan's first line of attack against Jesus, while the Lord was fasting in the desert, was to challenge His identity.

"If you are the Son of God command this stone to become bread." Luke 4:3

Only days earlier, Jesus and many eyewitnesses heard a voice from heaven "which said, 'You are my beloved son; in You I am well pleased.'" (Luke 4:21) The matter of identity had been established in Jesus' heart. He knew who He was and how His Father felt towards Him. Satan did not have a chance.

The same declaration is made repeatedly over us throughout the Bible. Romans says, "the Spirit Himself bears witness with our spirit that we are children of God...heirs of God and joint heirs with Christ." (Romans 8:16, 17) Paul wrote to the church at Ephesus that God has "predestined us to adoption as sons by Jesus Christ to Himself." (Ephesians 1:5) Paul affirmed the Galatians saying, "You are all sons of God through faith in Christ Jesus." (Galatians 3:26) John declared God gave to "as many as received Him...the right to become children of God." (John 1:12)

We belong to God. He created us. We are His children. He loves us! Before our Father gave us a body, by which we would function on earth as agents of transformation, God gave us a spirit with the capacity to commune and have fellowship with Him.

Overcoming the fear of man is the most significant internal victory required for pure operation within God's government. We overcome by knowing our identity in God and maintaining an intimate relationship with Him. The chief reason why Nehemiah, Jeremiah, and the Lord Jesus were neither intimidated, nor seduced by man was their solid stand in their identity as God's children and His ambassadors on the earth.

We can walk that way as well. We must!

Chapter 6

Increase
and
Relevance

Every seed is inherently equipped with the capacity for increase. One seed can bring forth remarkable growth, as long as it properly adapts to its environment.

In the Book of Revelation, the Apostle John declares that all glory and dominion in heaven and earth eternally belong to Jesus, "who loved us and washed us from our sins in His own blood, and has made us kings and priests to His God and Father." (Revelation 1:5-6)

Consider the same verse with added emphasis on the last conjunction: "[He] loved us...washed us from our sins...and has made us kings *and* priests." Jesus shed His blood for us, and God extended grace to us, not only so we could escape the torment of hell, but also to make us kings and priests unto Him. When we were born again, we entered God's Kingdom as the kings over whom Jesus Christ is King.

Peter perceived God's people as "a chosen generation, a royal priesthood" (1 Peter 2:9). In his letter to Timothy, Paul referred to Jesus as "the only Potentate, the King of kings and Lord of lords" (1 Timothy 6:15). Moreover, Revelation 19:16 states that the title, "King of kings and Lord of lords" is forever imprinted on Jesus' thigh. Clearly, the Lord has commissioned us and has made provision for us to release His Kingdom on earth, as both kings *and* priests unto Himself.

The transformation of communities, regions and nations is, in large part, contingent upon individuals recognizing they are God's kings and priests, and operating as such. In other words, our contribution in the discipleship and governance of nations depends on how well we exercise the kingly and priestly power and authority God has granted us.

Generally, the Church has done better in developing the priestly, than the kingly. Many churches focus on establishing systems for teaching, discipleship, evangelism, benevolence, and even the administration of spiritual gifts (healing, faith, miracles, prophecy). Fewer churches equip people to leverage their resources, spiritual gifts and training to serve (beyond the church) as God's chancellors; as ambassadors to a generation.

A local body of believers or a movement which devotes most of its energy and resources to attracting and developing "priests" will not appeal to many "kings"; therefore, it will most likely not maximize its potential in resources, creativity, leadership, influence, and ultimately impact. Church leaders, who develop the priestly but neglect the kingly in their organizations, are like scientists with brilliant inventions, but without the connections and financial backing needed for production, promotion and distribution.

After Jesus' death, Joseph of Arimathea went to Pilate to ask for the body of Jesus. He offered to bury the Lord in the tomb he had already built for himself (common practice among the wealthy of that day). Pontius Pilate immediately conceded. The governor would have never released Jesus' dead body to Christ's disciples (priestly). In fact, he ordered that a stone be placed in the entrance to the tomb, and guards be stationed there to keep the disciples *from* Jesus.

The Lord's body was given to Joseph, because when he approached Pilate, he operated in a kingly capacity. This wealthy, respected leader was as much a follower of Jesus as the disciples, but he remained quiet about his faith (strategic discretion). At the appropriate moment, Joseph demonstrated his devotion to Christ and his commitment to the Cause by leveraging his kingly influence to obtain the body.

Every Kingdom movement and operation that seeks to produce agents of transformation in the days ahead must maintain a proper balance in building up both the priestly and kingly among its constituents.

One note: The terms "king" and "priest" do not refer to actual positions of authority, i.e. a ruler over a kingdom or a spiritual leader in the church. The kingly and the priestly are internal attributes — modes of operation--God has instilled in us to help govern and serve our generation.

~~~

History, and particularly the life and reign of kings and rulers, can be very enlightening as it pertains to the government of God. The Bible makes it clear that regardless of the political and sociological scenarios out of which rulers emerge, ultimately it is God who gives kings power and authority on earth.

> *There is no authority except from God, and the authorities that exist are appointed by God.*
> Romans 13:1

Throughout history, certain elements of kingly rule seem to be common denominators with every king and kingdom, regardless of the time period, region, or individual gifting. The Book of Proverbs presents a number of shared kingly characteristics:

- Kings reign and decree justice by wisdom (8:15)

- Kings show favor towards the wise, and wrath against troublemakers (14:35)
- Kings' thrones are established by righteousness (16:12)
- Kings delight in right lips, and love those who speak what is right (16:13)
- A king's wrath is deadly; only wise men can appease them (16:14)
- A king's favor is like a cloud releasing latter rain (16:15)
- Kings' wrath is like a roaring lion; their favor like the dew of grass (19:12)
- Whoever provokes a king sins against his own life (20:2)
- Mercy, truth and kindness will preserve and uphold a king's throne (20:28)
- Kings befriend those who have pure hearts and grace on their lips (22:11)
- Those who excel in their work will stand before kings (22:29)
- It is the glory of kings to search out matters that God conceals (25:2)
- The heart of kings is unsearchable (25:3)
- Kings' thrones are established when the wicked are removed from their kingdoms (25:5)
- People must never exalt themselves in the presence of kings (25:6)
- Kings establish the land by justice, not corruption (29:4)
- The thrones of kings who judge the poor fairly will be established forever (29:14)
- A king marching with his troops is a stately and majestic sight (30:31)

- Kings must not give themselves to women or drunkenness, for such vices will pervert justice (31:3,4)

Consolidating the information above, we can conclude that kings and rulers who serve their people well, share the following:

1. They highly esteem and continually seek wisdom and understanding.
2. They are committed to distributing assistance to the poor, and justice for the oppressed.
3. They demand and uphold high levels of excellence.
4. They hold themselves to a higher standard than the rest of the people; therefore, they strive to rule with integrity.
5. Their high office demands respect and obedience from their constituents. Their executive power must be taken seriously.

Kingly leaders also continually endeavor to grow and advance their realms of influence and authority. They place a high value on increase, knowing full well that when progress and development cease, stagnation and deterioration follows.

> *In a multitude of people is a king's honor, but in the lack of people is the downfall of a prince.*
> Proverbs 14:28

Rulers recognize that their prominence and position depends, in large part, on their following. The largest component in any kingdom is its population; the most *significant* component is leadership that understands the importance of establishing a realm that enables existing inhabitants to thrive and multiply, while also drawing new people.

All US sports leagues air commercials throughout the year, in which they express thanks to the sport's fans. Moreover, every championship team owner, coach or captain, who lifts up a trophy in triumph, acknowledges, "We couldn't have done this without our fans!"

Good leaders make for good governments and growing kingdoms; thus, for increasing populations, revenues and opportunities for advancement. In order to lead well, leaders must structure their realms with the understanding that the growth and expansion of their operations are imperative for prosperity and longevity.

The principles of kingdom advancement did not emerge from monarchies, dynasties, empires, or business conglomerates; they originate from God's heart. Isaiah prophesied the Child who would be born to us—Jesus— "multiplied the nation and increased its joy". As Jesus demonstrated through His life and legacy, the multiplication of a nation hinges on sound leadership, proper administration, just distribution, and the enforcement of good laws. Nations multiply when there is proper government in place. The telephones in the immigration offices of oppressive nations never "ring off the hook." No one wants to move where there is bad government.

Isaiah also proclaimed there would be no end "of the *increase* of His government and peace."(emphasis mine) Our God is deliberate and passionate about progress, growth, multiplication and advancement. His Kingdom is based on Christ's good government; therefore, it is intrinsically equipped with the capacity for increase.

Jesus once likened the Kingdom of God to a mustard seed, "which indeed is the least of all the seeds." He said a man took that small seed and sowed it in his field. Though small and seemingly insignificant at first, when the mustard seed grew, it became "greater than the herbs and [became] a tree." (Matthew 13:31-32) Over time, the tree shot out large branches so that the birds of the air could nest under its shade.

Within the tiny mustard seed was the DNA for the largest tree in the field; the tree that would be sought for cover by wandering birds.

Just like the seed, God's Kingdom may initially seem limited by human measures. Mary's Baby in the manger at Bethlehem was as helpless and vulnerable as any other child on the earth; yet, He was destined to be the greatest Man who ever lived. Joseph and Mary had to provide for all His needs; but for all eternity, He would be the One by whom God "shall supply all [our] need according to His riches and glory."(Philippians 4:19) Baby Jesus had to be rushed to Egypt to protect Him from Herod's murderous sword; but, within just a few decades, He would emerge as King of kings. Every knee will bow to Him and every tongue will confess He is Lord. And "the kingdoms of this world [will] become the kingdoms of our Lord and He shall reign forever and ever!" (Revelation 11:15)

Most notable Kingdom endeavors begin small. One can never determine the potential of a person, organization, business, or ministry by applying human measuring standards. The internal qualities, which ultimately thrust individuals and organizations to notoriety, have a key similarity with the components that turn seeds to trees: They develop in obscurity for a long time.

Jesus' kingly and priestly qualities remained "hidden" for three decades. At age thirty, He walked up to John at the

Jordan River and asked to be baptized. The heavens parted, the Spirit descended on Him like a dove, and the Father declared, "This is my beloved Son in whom I am well pleased" (Matthew 3:17). Jesus spent the next forty days in the desert, where He overcame all of satan's temptations. Then, He "returned in the power of the Spirit to Galilee, and news of Him went out through all the surrounding region." (Luke 4:14) Jesus' time of hiding was over. The world was about to witness the seeds of the Kingdom inside Jesus exploding into giant trees. It was time for increase!

~~~

We don't know of any instances when Jesus engaged in promotional or fund-raising activities. No billboards, no website, no email blasts. No admonitions for folks to bring their friends to the meetings. Yet, Jesus always attracted large crowds.

At the outset of His ministry, the Lord even tried to limit His reputation by telling people specifically not to talk about Him. His requests and directives were not honored. It amazes me that the same Jesus, who as we saw earlier, quickly attracted a group of disciples by simply telling them to leave their nets and follow Him, could not get people to keep a secret about His whereabouts and operations.

With the exception of the few leaders who openly opposed Jesus, His authority and stature always moved people to submission and obedience. Only a handful of times in the four gospels do we find anyone disobeying His commands. Many people may have rejected Him; others may have left Him when they could not connect with the revelation He was releasing, but they were not blatantly disobedient.

But when Jesus "strictly warned" a man who had just been healed of leprosy, "See that you say nothing to anyone," the man "went out and began to proclaim it freely, and to spread the matter." This scenario played out often; consequently, Jesus could not even hold meetings in cities, "but was outside in deserted places; and they came to Him from every direction"! (Mark 1:43-45)

During our staff meetings, there has never been a time when we discussed a strategy to keep people from coming to our services and conferences. Not once have any of our folks ever told someone who has been healed or delivered to keep quiet about their breakthrough so the word of their miracle doesn't get out. In fact, with folks' permission, we broadcast as many testimonies as possible. We *want* people to become familiar with God's work among us. We *want* to draw a crowd; we desire increase!

Jesus and the early Church modeled the most effective way for churches and movements to grow: By continually seeking the presence of God and then manifesting His wisdom, grace, power and love. Consistent and sustainable growth is directly related to increase in the manifestation of God's glory.

Jesus could not contain the growth of His ministry, even when He expressly forbade people from talking about Him. No matter what they were told to say or not say, do or not do, people were drawn to the God who was operating in and through Jesus.

Another significant factor in Jesus' popularity was relevance. Jesus, the Carrier of God's government, continually increased in stature and influence, because the power of God attracted those who needed God, and the wisdom of God enabled Jesus to be relevant and appealing towards them.

With the exception of the unbelieving ruling elite—the Pharisees, scribes, teachers, elders--Jesus had an astounding ability to connect with people from every walk of life. Even beyond His profound teachings and miraculous works, Jesus touched lives and attracted respect, admiration, devotion and support from very diverse groups of people.

Men and women of all ages, children, tax collectors, small business owners, the rich and poor, Roman governmental and military leaders, Jewish religious leaders (the few who sought Him—like Nicodemus), farmers, outcasts (lepers and demoniacs, beggars, prostitutes, "winebibbers", fishermen, family, close friends, His disciples, Jews, Greeks, Samaritans, travelers from Tyre and Sidon—Jesus related to everyone just the same.

Jesus appealed to people, not just as a rabbi or a prophet, but as a well-rounded, fascinating individual. Jesus, the Man, was the greatest sign and wonder, more so than all the miracles, healings and deliverances He performed.

He taught in a way people could understand, using metaphors, allegories, parables and illustrations; all drawn from his listeners' backgrounds and surroundings.

A farmer sowed seed in a field...

A Pharisee and a tax collector went to pray...

The Kingdom is like...a pearl, a field, a mustard seed...

A man had two sons...

Don't throw pearls before swine...

You are salt, light, a city on a hill...

There were five wise virgins; five foolish...

Put new wine into new wineskins...

An enemy sowed tares in a man's wheat field...

Beware of the leaven of the Pharisees...

From the moment Jesus opened His mouth to speak, He had them. Eyes were fastened on Him; hearts were agreeing; spirits were bearing witness to what He was saying. It made sense. They could remember it. They could apply it. For the first time in a very long time, people were excited about receiving spiritual instruction. "Church" wasn't boring anymore; and neither was it confined to a building. It could spontaneously erupt along the seashore, on someone's doorstep, on a hillside, at the table. Jesus masterfully and magnificently reached people right where they were, with a message and mode of delivery that maximized His effectiveness.

He had them; and not only because He performed miracles. He was relevant!

Being relevant throughout the seasons and changes is imperative for sustained positive growth and expansion. One of the Church's greatest challenges in the days ahead is to remain current and relevant. The rhetoric and methods that were effective in past moves of God may limit our influence in today's world. Spiritual talk altogether may be completely inappropriate as a means to establish connection in certain settings and among some groups of people.

Over the years, we have been blessed with strategic God-ordained relationships with prominent leaders from various segments of society. I assure you, most of the conversations by which those relationships have been established and continue to grow did not feature much--if any--"Christian talk". It is important to connect with people where they are, and not try to push them where we want them to be. We don't always need to "witness" to them, "sneak in" the gospel message, or make sure they know "where we stand" on different issues. Being Christians does not make us experts in all matters of morality, anyway; and neither does it demand the constant declaration of our values in front of those who don't share them. Mature Christ-followers, who are secure in their identity and faith, are free to connect with non-believers within any context. And I promise you, they are the ones who are most effective in reaching people for Jesus!

Whenever my wife and I are invited to social gatherings where we meet new people, there seems to be a pattern for the way our interactions progress. Generally, we introduce ourselves or are introduced by our hosts to individuals, couples or small groups. While we all mingle and partake of hors d'oeuvres (my favorite moments), we share small talk and light conversation.

During those early moments of interaction, Danielle and I try to find as many non-ministry related areas as possible to connect with our new acquaintances. We are both widely-read. We obtained degrees in the secular fields of history and psychology. Moreover, we stay abreast of developments in business, finance, technology, social trends, sports, international news, environmental matters, etc. We are very deliberate to grow in our learning, so we can speak intelligently about as many subjects as possible.

Invariably, there comes a moment at these gatherings, when our new companions inquire, "What do you do for a living?" Almost every person who asks that question expresses surprise when we say we are pastors of a church.

The connections we make with the people through our input in subjects that interest them open a door for deeper conversation. What usually follows is a barrage of faith-related questions, which gives us opportunity to share Kingdom principles and God's love. By the time such events are finished, we even have the chance to minister to individuals, personally.

The key is establishing credibility by being genuine and relevant; and that stems from having the right sense of identity. We do not think of ourselves as ministers, but "sons" — in relationship with our Father and King before the foundations of the earth were laid. He chose us and commissioned us to live in this age and to serve our generation.

With the right identity and proper understanding of our assignment, we "live and move and have our being" in God. We are neither intimidated by man; nor desirous of man's approval. We walk confidently, yet humbly. We reveal His wisdom and love. We make God interesting and desirable to those He places in our path, by connecting with them right where we find them.

CHAPTER 7:

CROWD CONTROL

But the chief priests and elders persuaded the multitudes that they should ask for Barabbas and destroy Jesus.

Matthew 27:20

Right outside the city of Jerusalem, a "very great multitude" received Jesus, exclaiming, "Hosanna to the Son of David!" Upon His arrival, "all the city was moved," and people asked who He was. The multitude referred to Him as "Jesus, the prophet from Nazareth of Galilee." (Matthew 21:8-11).

Within just a few days, arguably many of the same Jerusalem folks raised their fists and shouted intensely, "Let Him be crucified!" (Matthew 27:22). The crowd that had hailed Jesus as a prophet and even Messiah (by their reference to Him being the Son of David), quickly turned into the mob which demanded His execution among thieves.

What precipitated such a radical change of position for the people of Jerusalem? What dynamic could possibly cause such a large contingent of the capital city's population to seek the release of a convicted murderer, Barabbas, over Jesus, who had only done right by everyone who knew Him?

Crowd control!

~~~

Every crowd is comprised of three main groups of people: Spectators, fans and followers. Spectators join the crowd to check out an event and/or the individual(s) speaking, per-forming, ministering, etc. Their chief motivation is curiosity or interest, stemming either from what they may have heard about the event, or from the flurry of activity and excitement surrounding it. A crowd always draws a crowd, so many spectators simply follow the crowd, seeking and inquiring what the hubbub is all about. Spectators often have no commitment or connection to the speaker or performer carrying the event.

I enjoy being a spectator at impromptu street performances in large cities, such as Boston and New York. I gravitate to the gathering crowd, weave through people to obtain a good vantage point, and watch. If I am moved by the performance, I commit spare change or small bills to the "hat"; if not, I walk away and soon forget about the matter.

Fans are informed and most likely have experience regarding the event and the person(s) at center stage. Sooner or later, fans also commit time and resources to attend such events. For instance, classical music fans purchase tickets, make plans and figure out logistics to attend symphony performances. They join crowds of other fans, as well as spectators and followers; and with each experience, they add to their understanding of and appreciation for the various aspects of symphony music. Fans may be former spectators or instant enthusiasts; either way, they become fans because whoever or whatever is drawing them to the events is enjoyable, entertaining and/or inspiring.

Followers are fans who demonstrate a higher degree of commitment and devotion. I recently met a man who shared his experience of attending the last Super Bowl Championship, in which his favorite team played (and lost). He had to fly to the host city (two plane changes), rent a car, stay in a hotel, eat out, and pay for parking--and he hadn't even entered the stadium yet. The ticket price was upwards of two thousand dollars--for average seats! Besides the disappointment of his team's loss, the event cost the man thousands of dollars and much time away from work. At the end of his sharing, he smiled and said, "I'd do it again gladly." Obviously, this man is not just a spectator or a fan, but a follower.

The team, band, speaker, musician, or minister that followers follow, influences their behavior; even their philosophy or world-view. It is not unusual to see followers of certain bands or movie franchises dressing like and imitating the behavior of their favorite musicians, singers or movie characters. Because of their openness and connection to their "stars", followers receive a degree of impartation from them.

At any given time, Jesus spoke and ministered to crowds of spectators, fans and followers. The Lord's anointing and charisma, as well as His ability to relate to people turned spectators to followers, almost immediately. Undoubtedly, many folks were fans, but for the most part, Jesus' crowds were comprised of "pre-followers" and followers. It was only a matter of minutes or hours before spectators opened their hearts to Jesus and chose to follow Him into the realms of the Kingdom He was proclaiming. Those who followed Jesus soon realized they were citizens of God's Kingdom, agents of transformation on the earth, and eventually part of a "great cloud of witnesses".

Christ-followers are not just highly committed members of a crowd; they are worshipers. Jesus' influence on their lives evokes wholehearted worship for the Living God — Father, Son and Holy Spirit. Christ-followers can connect with Jesus through worship, even when they are in a setting that is completely new to them. I have always felt very comfortable in numerous churches around the world. The languages and settings were different than what I was familiar with; however, my devotion to the Lord, and especially His presence, immediately united me with my brothers and sisters in worship.

The religious leaders of Jesus' day could not attract that kind of following; and they most certainly did not inspire people to worship God in spirit and truth. Their crowds were not comprised of spectators, fans or followers; rather of people who attended services out of habit or obligation; folks who had been relegated to "subjects" of an oppressive government, through manipulation and control--*crowd control.*

The problem for the Pharisees, priests and their cohorts was that their subjects were increasingly becoming spectators, fans, followers and ultimately worshipers of Jesus. Jesus' revolutionary, life-transforming words and ways were enlightening the oppressed. The principles governing God's Kingdom appealed to them. More importantly, His teachings were accompanied and validated by demonstrations of phenomenal authority and power. Astounding miracles affirmed everything Jesus was declaring.

The leaders who opposed Jesus were not only offended by His teachings; they were infuriated by His ever-increasing following. They knew it was only a matter of time before they would lose their power base. It was time to tighten the vice on Israel and get the crowds under control, literally.

Turning the crowds away from Jesus was no easy task. The priests were well aware of His good image and widespread receptivity among the masses. Any impulsive move on their part could mean disaster. That dynamic is well illustrated by an incident in which the Pharisees tried to trip up Jesus with questions in front of the crowd He was teaching. Jesus answered all the tricky questions well, and then told parables to expose His enemies' motives. The chief priests "perceived that He was speaking of them."

> *But when they sought to lay hands on Him, they feared the multitudes, because they took him for a prophet.* Matthew 21:45-46

Sooner or later, playing to the crowd leads to being played *by* the crowd. The Jewish leaders' use of manipulation worked against them. In a fear-driven society, fear works on both ends. Those who partner with fear and use it to impose their will on others will eventually come under fear's vicious grip themselves. It's like working for the Mob—once you join, you can never get out without a bruising. I was once taught by a professor who likened the use of intimidation for the purpose of control, to riding a tiger. His punch line: "Eventually you have to get off the beast; and how do you do so without getting eaten?"

~~~

As we will see in more detail below, crowds have amazing capacity to establish, influence and shift environments. Politicians know that well. If they can move a crowd in a certain direction, they can maintain or change the status quo, accordingly. Election, re-election, the passage of laws, fiscal reforms, and the introduction of new rhetoric often depend on leaders' ability to impact and mobilize crowds.

Man's government relies, in large part, on attracting and "working" crowds; as well as in keeping crowds interested, motivated, and satisfied. The crowd gives leaders influence; but then it exerts influence on them.

The government of God operates differently. God does not play *to* the crowd, but *for* the crowd. He does not try to win supporters by doing what they want; God does what *He* wants, which is always what is best for us. All of God's directives, laws and commands are ultimately for our benefit. Those who recognize God's love and care, gladly surrender to Him and join His "crowd".

Jesus, as "Chief Executive Carrier" of God's government on earth, did not operate according to the expectations or wishes of crowds; only by the will of His Father, which was to save, heal, restore and empower individuals.

Jesus only did what His Father was doing, and spoke what His Father was speaking; and because all of God's actions and words were designed to benefit people, crowds were drawn to Jesus. The Lord never tried to gather a crowd; He simply preached the gospel of the Kingdom and revealed the Father's heart. Then, crowds of people flocked to Him and grew in numbers, exponentially!

There is a vast difference between needing the crowd and leading the crowd. Jesus never needed the crowd. The way He led attracted followers of every sort. Some followed Him everywhere and provided for Him out of their substance. Twelve became His disciples, and lived with Him. Seventy-two others were a broader circle of co-laborers. The religious elite did not attract any followers; therefore, they *needed* the crowd in order to get their agenda across.

Our Kingdom assignments require focus and commitment to God's will and plan. As in the case of Jesus, it is most challenging to stay on track during moments or seasons of success.

Achievement is usually accompanied with noise—the sound of accolades, congratulations, celebration. Family, friends, small or large crowds cheer us on:

"Go pro!" "Pursue another degree!" "Accept the offer!" "Sign up with the label!" "Take the job!" "Start your ministry!" "Buy a boat!" "Build bigger barns!"

It is tempting in that environment to deviate from the purposes of God—even though our success is part of His master plan for our lives—and yield to the prompting of the crowd. Jesus' temptation in the desert was intense, yet very brief. The pressure by His followers to be crowned king and meet their expectations was constant. The roar of approval from favorable crowds is often more menacing than the loneliness of our desert experiences.

> *Now when it was day, He departed and went into a deserted place. And the crowd sought Him and came to Him, and tried to keep Him from leaving them; but He said to them, "I must preach the kingdom of God to the other cities also, because for this purpose I have been sent."* Luke 4:42-43

Desert or mountaintop; among friends or foes, the Lord set His "face like a flint" towards destiny. We are called to the same!

~~~

The crowds favored Jesus, and His last visit to Jerusalem extenuated the problem. People were coming out in droves to meet Him in the outskirts of the city. They were laying down palm leaves and garments. They were calling Him the Son of David. Even so, Israel's leaders were careful not to make any moves on Jesus prematurely, lest the crowds turn against them.

Even when the Lord openly confronted the Pharisees and their colleagues, they chose to walk away. They could not touch Jesus yet, because the crowd was for Him.

Even towards the end of Jesus' life--when the plot "to take Jesus by trickery and kill Him" was in high gear--Christ's enemies were very calculating about the time and place of His arrest, "lest there be an uproar among the people." (Matthew 26:4,5)

Any civil disturbance would have resulted in the involvement of the Roman army to keep the peace. Consequently, the conspirators would lose credibility with the governor, whose upcoming role in the plot was pivotal. They did not stir the waters until the time was ripe; until they could leverage their positions and resources to influence the crowds, and ultimately the Roman government, in their favor. When that time came, Christ's enemies drew from their understanding of fundamental crowd dynamics to turn the tide.

Fundamentally, a crowd is a number of people gathered together, because of common interests, objectives or causes.

Crowds may be large or small; and they may be constituted by individuals from very diverse ethnic, racial, cultural and socio-economic backgrounds. Nonetheless, once men and women join a crowd that represents their interests, objectives or cause, they lose their individual sound and initiative. They think as the crowd thinks; they speak as the crowd speaks; they act as the crowd acts. Crowds gain momentum (for good or evil) when individual voices in the crowd become unified and synchronized to pursue the same things, for the same cause, at the same time.

The noise of the crowd drowns out any individual voice that speaks contrary to what the crowd agrees upon; therefore, saying anything that could be deemed a diversion from the crowd's general mindset is unthinkable. When in a crowd, "going with the flow" rules the day.

One strong, charismatic, well-spoken leader, or a small minority of leaders, can direct a crowd. The book of Acts abounds with examples. While Paul and Barnabas ministered in Antioch, the word of God spread from the synagogue where they first preached, "throughout all the region." (Acts 13:49) Their message appealed more to the Gentiles, who "were glad and glorified the word of the Lord."

> *But when the Jews saw the multitudes, they were filled with envy.* Acts 13:45

Consequently, a small detachment of Jews "stirred up the devout and prominent women and the chief men of the city," who incited "persecution against Paul and Barnabas and expelled them from their region." (Acts 13:50)

In another incident at Philippi, Paul and Silas were deemed troublemakers after Paul cast out a spirit of divination from a slave girl. When her fortune-telling craft was terminated and "her masters saw that their hope of profit was gone," they apprehended the apostles and dragged them to the authorities.

The small number of magistrates pronounced Paul and Silas guilty of "exceedingly troubling [the] city."

> *Then the multitude rose up together against them.* Acts 16:19, 20, 22

Under certain circumstances, an individual or a small group can also shift the opinion, position and direction of a crowd, rather quickly. The evil queen, Jezebel--wife of Ahab, King of Israel--used her position of authority to plant two "scoundrels...to bear false witness" against a righteous man, Naboth. Her goal was to eliminate Naboth and give his vineyard to her husband, who wanted that plot of land. With Jezebel's backing, the two false witnesses lied about Naboth and turned the entire city against him.

> *Then they took [Naboth] outside the city and stoned him with stones so that he died.* 1 Kings 21:13

Crowds are easily turned when seeds of accusation, doubt or suspicion are planted by powerful and influential leaders. Those were the seeds sown by Jesus' enemies to convert a large, stable crowd of Christ-followers to the volatile mob that demanded His execution.

Crowds turn into mobs when they are emotionally stirred. Emotions run high when crowds are inspired by good speakers, motivated by great causes, and especially when crowds face conditions of danger. The religious leaders could never move crowds by signs, wonders, miracles, or inspired teachings— spiritual gifting and revelation had been long gone. The only emotions available to motivate the crowd for their purposes were fear and anger—products of the threats and coercion on the part of the Jewish elite.

In the next chapter, we examine in more detail the tactics by which Jesus' enemies used fear and anger for crowd control--the last and most essential element of their manifold, three-year plot.

CHAPTER 8:

THE PLOT UNFOLDS

Then the chief priests, the scribes, and the elders of the people assembled at the palace of the high priest, who was called Caiaphas, and plotted to take Jesus by trickery and kill Him.

Matthew 26:3-4

The final phase of the plot to destroy Jesus was involved and multi-faceted. The conspirators' dastardly objective could only be attained if the following components aligned perfectly:

1) The necessary political maneuvering to secure a Roman military force for Jesus' arrest.
2) A crowd of brainwashed or coerced Jews to accompany the Roman soldiers; thus, ensuring strength in numbers in the event of a confrontation with Jesus' disciples.
3) Assurance Jesus could be found quickly once the arrest-party was assembled.
4) Absence of a large crowd of Jesus-followers during the arrest — to avoid unnecessary disturbance and the loss of Roman governmental support.
5) Finding individuals to falsely testify against Jesus.
6) A speedy trial and verdict to prevent word of Jesus' arrest spreading to Jesus' supporters.
7) Turning the multitude of Jerusalem locals and Passover visitors against Jesus.
8) Convincing Pontius Pilate to order Jesus' execution.

Finding Jesus' place of abode was priority. The conspirators needed someone with inside knowledge of His whereabouts. Somehow, word got out that the priests were looking for an informant. It did not take long for the fish to bite.

From the very beginning, not only of Jesus' life, but of all mankind, satan operated through anyone who would host him to stage opposition, resistance, interference, and ultimately the destruction, not only of the Anointed One, but of all people whose lives were committed to God.

Like heat-seeking missiles, demonic forces locked onto the dry places in men's hearts, such as the power-hunger and greed of the Jewish leaders; the political ambitions of Herod and Pontius Pilate; people's lust for glory and fame; the fear of man--in essence, every attitude and motive that "exalts itself above the knowledge of God." (2 Corinthians 10:5)

Individuals whose morals and ethics are compromised tend to think and operate similarly. It's only a matter of time before their character flaws lead them to connect and collaborate with others like them.

The same satanic forces operating in the leaders determined to kill the Son of God, worked within one of His closest confidants, Judas Iscariot.

Judas' motive made for a simple case of hiring a traitor. He wanted money and the privilege of being granted "a detachment of troops and officers...with lanterns, torches, and weapons." (John 18:3). Greed and self-importance – stemming from pride – are among the most prevalent and easily-exploitable weaknesses throughout history.

Judas asked for his bounty, and the chief priests "counted out to him thirty pieces of silver." From that moment on, Judas "sought opportunity to betray Him." (Matthew 26:14-16)

Betraying Jesus and turning Him over to His accusers involved another contemptible quality Judas shared with the religious authorities, hypocrisy.

Judas would lead "the multitude with swords and clubs" to the place where Jesus stayed. Then, he would approach, greet and kiss Jesus; thereby, denoting the suspect to the arrest party. Thus, while on hire by Jesus' enemies, Judas would express intimate friendship towards Him. It was the very same mode of hypocrisy by which the Pharisees, scribes, priests, and elders operated. While posing as godly defenders of the faith before the people, they secretly connived and conspired to kill God's Son. Like Judas, they acted as close friends of God, while in partnership with the enemy.

~~~

In the middle of the night, while Jerusalem slept, the detachment of Roman soldiers and Jewish escort led Jesus from the Garden of Gethsemane to Caiaphas, the high priest, where the scribes and elders had assembled.

Next on the checklist was finding enough evidence to convict Jesus of a crime punishable by death. It was a tall order.

> *Now the chief priests and all the council sought testimony against Jesus to put Him to death, but found none.* Mark 14:55

False witnesses lined up to testify, "but their testimonies did not agree."(vs. 56) Exasperated, the high priest questioned Jesus directly, hoping he might get Him to confess to wrongdoing. At first, the Lord remained silent, but when asked if He was "the Christ, the Son of the Blessed", He broke the stalemate:

> "I am. And you will see the Son of Man sitting at the
> right hand of the Power, and coming with the clouds
> of heaven." Mark 14:62

The conspirators rejoiced, thinking Jesus had played right into their hands:

> "What further need do we have of witnesses? You
> have heard the blasphemy!"...And they all condemned
> Him to be deserving of death. Mark 14:63-64

To the Pharisees, priests and elders, all the pieces of the plot appeared to be moving into position like the clouds of a "perfect storm". The arrest had gone off without a glitch; the quick arraignment and conviction followed. Everything was falling into place. Now for the final act: Getting the Roman government to send Jesus to the cross.

First thing the next morning, the chief priests, elders, scribes and the entire council "bound Jesus, led Him away, and delivered Him to Pilate." (Mark 15:1)

> We have a law, and according to our law He ought to
> die, because He made Himself the Son of God.
> John 19:7

Their law meant nothing to the Roman governor. None of Jesus' specified or unspecified infractions, including blasphemy, called for the death penalty. Pilate would not condemn Jesus for claiming He was the Son of God.

Not unless he was pressured to do so...

~~~

The next part of the plot involved two elements:

1) Pulling on the annual feast custom, whereby the governor released to the Jews a prisoner of their choice.
2) Influencing the crowd to ask for Barabbas, instead of Jesus.

Under the direction of the conspirators, "the multitude, crying aloud, began to ask [Pilate] to do just as he had always done for them." (Mark 15:8)

Knowing that "the chief priests had handed [Jesus] over because of envy", Pilate offered to release Jesus.

> But the chief priests stirred up the crowd, so that he should rather release Barabbas to them. (vs. 11)

Pilate, still finding no fault with Jesus, tried to reason with the crowd.

> What then do you want me to do with Him whom you call King of the Jews? (vs. 12)

The crowd cried, "Crucify Him!"

The more Pilate "sought to release Him," the louder the Jews became. Along with the crowd's demands for Christ's crucifixion came a serious threat:

> "If you let this Man go, you are not Caesar's friend. Whoever makes himself a king speaks against Caesar." John 19:12

On cue, the chief priests added, "We have no king but Caesar!" (vs. 15)

> *The voices of these men and of the chief priests prevailed. So Pilate gave sentence that it should be as they requested.* Luke 23:23-24

The use of fear and manipulation were the key to the plot's last phase. By leveraging their prominence and political power among the people, and by threatening with consequences for non-conformists, the religious elite stirred up fear in the people. Although I cannot prove this, I firmly believe many of the people outside Pilate's court were completely unfamiliar with Jesus or His ministry. They just went along with the rulers' demands, because they feared the Pharisees and priests.

As we saw previously, an atmosphere of danger turns crowds to mobs. The danger of being labeled as rebels and ostracized by the priests turned the tide. The crowd became a mob; one which had been coerced to shout against Jesus. Moreover, the mob projected their fear on Pilate, by threatening to report him as an enemy of Caesar.

Crowd control had worked well for the conspirators. The crowd did as it was instructed. Pilate responded as was expected. Barabbas was set free; and Jesus had been delivered to the Jews to be crucified.

~~~

The plot against Jesus was a plot to eliminate all influence from God's government on the earth. It was the result of the *government collision* that occurred when Jesus was sent to the world. David foresaw the entire plot hundreds of years before the Jewish leaders concocted it:

The kings of the earth set themselves, and the rulers take counsel together, against the LORD and against His anointed, saying, "Let us break Their bonds in pieces and cast away Their cords from us."
Psalm 2:2-3

David also described God's response to the plot:

He who sits in the heavens shall laugh. The LORD shall hold them in derision. Psalm 2:4

Then, God would "declare the decree":

"You are My Son, today I have begotten You. Ask of Me, and I will give you the nations for Your inheritance, and the ends of the earth for your possession."
Psalm 2:7-8

The plot that resulted in Christ's execution was catalytic for the fulfillment of God's Plan: Dominion would be granted to Jesus and to His followers, you and me!

~~~

The closer we get to Jesus' dying moment, the greater the contrast between two kingdoms. On one side, we see Jesus. He loved Judas, who betrayed Him; Peter, who denied Him; and the other ten disciples who fled for their lives. He performed a creative miracle in the garden to reattach Malchus' severed ear. He did not defend Himself when He was accused, confounding Pilate by His stature and temperance. Jesus held fast to His identity and wholeheartedly committed to God's will.

When He was reviled, [He] did not revile in return; when He suffered, He did not threaten, but committed Himself to Him who judges righteously 1 Peter 2:23

On the other side: The Pharisees, scribes, priests and elders. They intensified their assault on Jesus through false witnesses and bogus accusations. They intimidated a crowd into switching sides. They sought the release of a murderer and the execution of God's Son. They threatened Pilate. They confessed Caesar as their only king. And while Jesus hung on the cross, "the rulers...sneered" (Luke 23:35).

> *The chief priests also mocking with the scribes and the elders said, "He saved others; Himself He cannot save."* Matthew 27:41-42

As the conspirators uncovered the final layers of their wicked plot, God revealed, through Jesus, the greatest facets of His wonderful plan for the redemption of mankind.

At the epitome of His suffering, Jesus prayed for His tormentors:

> *"Father forgive them, for they do not know what they do."* Luke 23:34

He made provision for His mother and His beloved disciple, John:

> *"Woman, behold your son!" Then he said to the disciple, "Behold your mother."* John 19:26,27

He released life and hope into one of the criminals hanging next to Him, when the man asked Jesus to remember him when He entered His Kingdom:

> *"Assuredly, I say to you, today you will be with Me in Paradise."* Luke 23:43

About the sixth hour, Jesus gave up His last breath with a final cry, "Father, into Your hands I commit My spirit."(Luke 23:46) Then, He died.

~~~

It looked as though the conspirators had won. Their plot was successful, indeed; but so was God's master plan. The moment Jesus breathed His last, mercy triumphed over judgment; truth prevailed over lies; love trumped hatred; righteousness defeated sin; resurrection life conquered death and the grave; and God won the ultimate victory over satan!

Man had a way to the Father. Through Jesus, he was granted eternal life in heaven and dominion in the earth!

> *He is despised and rejected by men,*
> *A Man of sorrows and acquainted with grief.*
> *And we hid, as it were, our faces from Him;*
> *He was despised, and we did not esteem Him.*
> *Surely He has borne our griefs*
> *And carried our sorrows;*
> *Yet we esteemed Him stricken,*
> *Smitten by God, and afflicted.*
> *But He was wounded for our transgressions,*
> *He was bruised for our iniquities;*
> *The chastisement for our peace was upon Him, And by*
> *His stripes we are healed.*
> Isaiah 53:3-5

CHAPTER 9:

STARTING AT THE END

The stone which the builders rejected has become the chief cornerstone.

Psalm 118:22

I wonder how the rest of the day and weekend went for Jesus' murderers.

For weeks, they had intensified efforts that had begun three years earlier. Brimming with self-righteousness, and convinced they were in the will of God, the rulers of Israel had applied their authority, influence, power, ability, and resources to see Jesus nailed to a cross. All their key objectives seemed to have been accomplished. Jesus was gone; His followers had scattered; and the multitudes were forcefully reminded who was boss.

One would expect the conspirators to have gathered, at least in small groups, to discuss the events. We can only imagine the conversation:

"Well, He's dead."

"Finally!"

"Whew--that was a close one! Pilate sure was a tough nut to crack."

"Good thing we turned that crowd around."

"Gentlemen, He's gone! We're back in business."

"That was quite a freaky storm, huh?"

"Yeah, they said it was an earthquake. The rocks split and some tombs were disturbed. I heard people came out of their graves and walked around."

"We're not touching that!"

"No more miracles; no more teachings; no more crowds; no more of His gospel-of-the-kingdom preaching."

"So much for destroying the temple and rebuilding it; though, the temple curtain did mysteriously rip around the time the earthquake happened."

"They found Judas dead in the potter's field. He hung himself."

"We'll buy the field with his bribe money. It's the right thing to do."

"I say we better keep tabs on Barabbas. He's loose now."

"Someone went to Pilate, asking for Jesus' body. They'll bury Him in that man's new tomb."

"I don't care who gets Him or where they bury Him; just make sure there's a stone in front of the tomb and guards watching it."

The next day, the chief priests and Pharisees paid Pilate a visit. Their tone was less intense than the previous time they had met; but demanding, nonetheless:

> *Command that the tomb be made secure until the third day, lest His disciples come by night and steal Him away.* Matthew 27:64

Pilate consented. He released a guard detail and authorized the Jews to do whatever they deemed necessary.

So they went and made the tomb secure, sealing the stone and setting the guard." Matthew 27:66

Right when Christ's enemies felt confident their schemes had finally brought an end to Him and His ways; Just when everything finally seemed to be going their way, to their shock and horror, the conspirators quickly discovered Jesus' end was only the beginning.

That Sunday morning, Jerusalem awoke to the rumbling of another earthquake. The population temporarily increased by one--an angel, who "descended from heaven, and came and rolled back the stone from the door." I don't know who this angel was, but his attitude makes him my favorite. After rolling away the stone, he "sat on it"! (Matthew 28:2)

The movement Jesus generated was far from being eradicated. And Jesus was not dead; not anymore! Over the next forty days, He would walk through walls, appear and disappear at will, cook fish for His disciples at dawn, and show Himself to hundreds of people. Afterwards, He would give His followers instructions about the next step, and He would ascend into heaven.

The Holy Spirit would take it from there.

The Jesus revolution was far from snuffed; it would spread like fire—everywhere! His government and peace would continue to get established in every corner of the world.

~~~

Shortly before His ascension, Jesus met with His disciples on a mountain. He said to them:

All authority has been given to Me in heaven and on earth. Go therefore and make disciples of all the nations. Matthew 28:18-19

Christ's authority and power came from His Father. During one of His last meetings with the disciples before His arrest, Jesus said everything the Father had was His; and it would soon be bestowed to each of them. The Holy Spirit would be the agent transferring Jesus' heavenly resources to His disciples.

He will take of Mine and declare it to you. John 16:14

Thus, all three members of the Godhead were involved in the disciples' endowment with the heavenly inheritance required for dominion. The Father gave everything He had to His son; Jesus passed on that inheritance by the Holy Spirit, to the apostles.

~~~

During a recent visit to Cyprus, my dad took me for a ride up the mountains to show me where my late grandmother lay (she had passed away a few months earlier). It was beautiful Saturday afternoon on the island; a perfect day for everything that transpired.

Our journey had begun in the coastal city of Larnaca, where my parents reside. Earlier that day, Mom, Dad, and I had driven forty minutes northeast to Agios Giorgios of Alamanou, where we met up with my aunt and uncle for a phenomenal meal of grilled octopus and squid. While we were finishing up at the restaurant, my dad thought he and I could head to the family burial plot at Agios Ioannis. My mom would return to Limassol with my aunt and uncle, and we would all reconvene at their penthouse patio later that evening.

As much as I was missing my wife and children (this was a personal trip), I was thoroughly enjoying my time with my family in Cyprus. The moments I got to share alone with my parents, siblings and extended family were priceless.

Dad and I drove east from the restaurant for about twenty minutes; then, turned north towards the mountains at the outskirts of Limassol. For the next hour or so, we followed the winding roads and took in the majestic scenery. Before us, lay the imposing Troodos Mountain Range; behind us, the breathtaking view of the Mediterranean Sea.

We talked lightly and enjoyably about everything under the sun: Politics, soccer, family, finances, education, etc.—a typical Cypriot father-son conversation. At one point in our ascent, my dad pointed to my left and said, "We own some land somewhere up there." It was news to me. Good to know.

A few minutes later, we came up to the village of Gerasa, my grandmother's birthplace. Again, my dad pointed to my left and informed me of another plot he inherited from his mother. We actually drove up to that field later in the day. I was thrilled to see numerous olive trees in it, and I was sure to make known my wishes for ownership of the tree I deemed most fruitful!

After many more twists and turns in our northward journey, we arrived at Agios Ioannis. My dad pulled over to show me a beautiful piece of land. It lay right off the road and had a river running through it. "That's ours too, as well as another plot way up there on that hill."

Wow! I didn't know our family owned that much land. I was excited! And a bit curious...

Within a few minutes, we were standing by my grand-mother's grave. I paid my respects. While Dad was busy look-ing for matches to light a votive candle, I fixed my gaze in the general direction of all the family plots I had learned about that day.

My face still turned towards the hills, I asked, "Dad, how did Giagia and Pappous (my grandparents) acquire those fields?"

"Much of that land was granted to their parents by the British during colonial times." (1899-1960)

"Granted by the British?" I am a student of history, and I grew up on the island. To my knowledge, British colonial rule in Cyprus was dictatorial and oppressive on many counts. How could there have been such generous land grants from those who ruled with an iron fist?

My dad said the British made an agreement with the village folk. If they worked the land for a number of years, the Crown would then turn the land over to them. Sure enough, my great grandfather tilled the land and planted crops, year after year, until he owned it. The excellent British land registry system recorded the acquisitions.

On August 16, 1960, the Zürich and London Agreement between the United Kingdom, Greece and Turkey declared Cyprus an independent republic, free from British rule. Soon, the British left the island. Their land registry system remained;

and so did all the transactions recorded during the time of occupation.

It was at that particular juncture of my dad's narrative that I received revelation:

My family's inheritance came out of what was arguably the most oppressive regime the nation had known. The "rod" of my grandfather's oppressor became the catalyst for my family's blessing!

Justice!

> Righteousness and **justice** are the foundation of Your throne; Mercy and truth go before Your face. (emphasis mine) Psalm 89:14.
>
> ~~~

The same dynamic played out in regards to our inheritance from Jesus.

Israel's leaders personified the vinedressers from one of Jesus' parables. (Matthew 21) That particular group of hirelings had inappropriately responded to the owner's repeated attempts to receive the fruit from his vineyard. Instead of sending back fruit to their employer, they dishonored every servant, whom the landowner sent. They "beat one, killed one, and stoned another..." (vs. 35)

> Again he sent other servants, more than the first, and they did likewise to them. (vs. 36)

Finally, the owner decided to send his own son to the vineyard. Even after everything the evil workers had done, the landowner still believed for the best.

They will respect my son. (vs. 37)

They didn't! The vinedressers saw the son coming and said:

This is the heir. Come let us kill him and seize his inheritance. (vs. 38)

The vinedressers made two huge mistakes:

1. Inheritances are given; not taken.
2. The son's father — the only one with authority to *give* the inheritance--was still alive!

The crimes and imprudence of the vinedressers were soon dealt with severely by the sword of the landowner. He destroyed "those wicked men miserably, and lease[d] his vineyard to other vinedressers who [rendered] to him the fruits in their seasons." (vs. 41)

The chief priests and Pharisees recognized that Jesus "was speaking of them." (vs. 45) Through the parable, Jesus was exposing the conspiracy of the religious and political elite. He was also pointing out their blunder. Just like the workers in the vineyard, Christ's enemies tried to seize and secure the inheritance they had lost by the hardness of their hearts and their godlessness.

For generations, the Pharisees, scribes and priests had re-sisted, killed and maimed the prophets who had been sent by the Father — just like the servants sent by the landowner. Now, they were conspiring against the very Son of God. But the in-heritance had not been given to them and the Father was very much alive. And after three days in a grave...so was the Son!

Generally, people receive inheritances after the ascendants (parents or relatives) die. God's inheritance was no different; it would only be released after Jesus died.

> *And for this reason He is the Mediator of the new covenant, by means of death...that those who are called may receive the promise of the eternal inheritance. For where there is a testament, there must also of necessity be the death of the testator. For a testament is in force after men are dead, since it has no power at all while the testator lives.*
> Hebrews 9:16-17

The conspirators' first—and worst—mistake was their notion that eliminating Jesus would secure their portion of the heavenly inheritance. By killing God's Son, they actually disqualified themselves completely from His inheritance, forever.

> *"Therefore I say to you, the kingdom of God will be taken from you and given to a nation bearing the fruits of it."* Matthew 21:43

Moreover, the death of Christ now made the inheritance available to His followers. He had to die in order to pass it on to us, and so by killing Him, the Pharisees and company made way for our greatest blessing! As a final blow, Jesus arose from the grave on the third day, by the power of the Holy Spirit—a portion soon to be added to the inheritance of the saints! (Ephesians 1:20)

As in the case of my family's land holdings procured from British rule, the despotic rule of the Pharisees, scribes, priests, and elders--and especially the culmination of their oppression through Christ's execution--brought forth the richest inheritance for God's family: Jesus—the Risen and Victorious Savior of the world!

All the resistance, reproach and persecution that results from the collision of governments--including the torture and murder of Christ-followers—will never be able to stop God's people from advancing His Kingdom. The Lord will always reverse the intent and effects of opposition and oppression to benefit His body, until God's inheritance is distributed to us and through us to every corner of the earth.

Until:

> *The kingdoms of this world [will] become the king-*
> *doms of our Lord and of His Christ, and He shall reign*
> *forever and ever!* **Revelation 11:15**

EPILOGUE
FATHER, HOLY SPIRIT...
AND SON!

Ever since I committed my life to God, I desired to encounter Jesus. I undoubtedly knew Him and loved Him. I bowed to Him as Savior and Lord, and I trusted Him with every aspect of my existence. Almost daily, for the last decade, I have read at least one chapter in the four gospels, beginning with Matthew, working my way through the last chapter of John, then starting all over again. I devoured anything Jesus had to say—the "red letters." Yet, I had not connected with Jesus in a personal way, as I had with the Father and the Holy Spirit.

In April of 1991, on a college campus in New Jersey, I first encountered God, the Father, in a dream. I dreamed I had died without living for Him; consequently, I was headed to a place of doom, apart from His presence. I woke up wet from perspiration, after pleading with the Father to grant me three more days to get my life in order. For the first time, I knew the God of the Bible was real. He was my Creator and Father, and He loved me. He wanted to have relationship with me, as a son. I immediately surrendered to Him. For many years after that episode, my prayers, dreams, thoughts, and desires revolved around knowing and pleasing the God I had encountered in the dream, the Father.

At the same time, I was yielded to and learning all I could about Jesus. I was filled with the Holy Spirit and recognized the grace by which the Spirit was changing the world, even through my own life and ministry; however, I only had a personal connection with the Father.

In May of 2008, I had a life-changing encounter with the Holy Spirit. While on a mission to Sydney, Australia, the Spirit of God overshadowed me on a Sunday morning. For the next three days, He spoke to my heart very clearly and openly, as a friend. For most of that time, I felt as though electricity was going through my brain. I was lightheaded and unable to walk farther than a few feet. Yet, I was comfortable, joyful, and full of peace. I knew this was a work of the Holy Spirit. Many things changed after that encounter.

My passion to know God's ways shot through the roof. Revelation in His word exploded within me. And, under strict orders from the Holy Spirit, I completely departed from written notes in my preaching. In every speaking engagement from that day forward, I would connect with the Holy Spirit as I did in Sydney, and He would co-labor with me to release the words the Father desired to share with His people. It has been frightening and exhilarating; a trust-walk with my Friend and Master, the Holy Spirit.

Still, no encounter with Jesus…

Over the last few years, I have longed for the moment when I would feel the same closeness and intimacy with Jesus, as I did with the Father and the Spirit. I believed God would grant me the desire of my heart. I knew it was only a matter of time before Jesus would manifest Himself to me. I often wondered what that encounter would entail. Perhaps seeing His face in a dream; hearing His audible voice during prayer; or watching Him walk through the walls of my office while I'm in worship. In all my imaginations, I never thought my most significant personal encounter with Jesus would come while writing a book; *this* book!

I did not see His face and I did not hear His voice. From the moment I decided to dedicate this work to Him, and determined to write Jesus' story from the perspective of the collision between His government and the world's, I have felt the glory of His presence and the eminence of His stature every step of the way.

The prevalent radiance of Jesus in the room has caused me to weep uncontrollably mid-sentence, many times. In other moments, the revelation of His wonderful love and mercy moved me to stop typing and to lift my hands in adoration. At times when the Spirit further enlightened me regarding Christ's splendor and majesty as supreme Potentate and Ruler over the nations, I would remain completely motionless, in awe of His overwhelming authority and power.

I have no idea how far *Government Collision* will circulate; or what impact it will have in the lives of its readers. I know it has immensely touched my life, because of the encounter I've had with the Son while writing it!

~~~

I'd like to take a personal moment to ask about your own approach to Jesus. If you were attending one of His powerful gatherings by the shores of Galilee or a hillside on the outskirts of Jerusalem, would you be a spectator, fan or follower?

Let's try to see this in our mind's eye together. You are sitting in that crowd, somewhere towards the back. You are positive about what is taking place. Jesus certainly has great content. He seems genuine and He sounds convincing. Even so, you are carefully listening and processing as a spectator, maybe even a fan--checking things out thoroughly before making any commitment.

Suddenly, Jesus begins to wade through the crowd. He's looking in your direction. The closer He gets, the more clear it becomes that His eyes are actually fixed on you. Don't be nervous; this is good!

Finally, He stops right in front of you. His eyes are full of love. His gaze penetrates layers of shame, disappointment, unworthiness and limitation. He does not judge your failures and shortcomings. He sees your future all the way to the farthest reaches of eternity. He knows there's a follower, a worshiper insider you.

He puts His hand on your shoulder. "Come follow me," He says. "Let's change the world together."

He desires to have you with Him. He wants to free you from the sins and bondages of your past. He longs to enrich and empower you; to immerse you in His extraordinary love. And He is ready to entrust a portion of His Kingdom's govern-ance to you.

It is by God's design and purpose that you are reading this page right now. He has ordered your steps to bring you to a place of decision.

Trust Jesus, friend! Open your heart to Him. Everything He is telling you is true!

From the deepest part of me, I encourage you to take the leap of faith into "follower status"--to commit your life to the Lord Jesus Christ.

If you are willing, I want to pray with you right now:

Jesus, I open my heart to You. I want You to come into my life. I desire to follow You. Forgive me of my sins and wash me clean. Show me Your ways and teach me how to live and serve in Your Kingdom. Use me for Your purposes. I want my life to count for You.

I believe in You, Jesus. Thank You for Your sacrifice. I receive You as Lord and Savior.

You are my King!

Amen.

Congratulations! I welcome you to the Kingdom of God in the Name of the Father, Holy Spirit and…Son!

I look forward to worshipping and serving alongside you. It will be an awesome time. You'll see!

Let's change the world with Jesus!

With Love,

Marios Ellinas

Contact Information:

Marios Ellinas
Valley Shore Assembly of God
36 Great Hammock Road
Old Saybrook, CT 06475

Email: <u>maellinas@yahoo.com</u>

To order more copies of this book, visit:

- <u>www.amazon.com</u>

- <u>www.mariosellinas.com</u>

Other books by Marios Ellinas:

- *Running to the Impossible* (2008)
- *Warrior Material* (2010)
- *The Next Test* (2011)

www.ingramcontent.com/pod-product-compliance
Lightning Source LLC
Chambersburg PA
CBHW061950070426
42450CB00007BA/1111